JOSEPHINE MOFFETT BENTON

A DOOR AJAR

FACING DEATH WITHOUT FEAR

The Pilgrim Press • *NEW YORK* • *PHILADELPHIA*

To my husband
Frederic Elmon Benton
without whose loving encouragement
none of my books
would have been written

Library of Congress Catalog Card Number 65-16442

79-109464

The publisher wishes to express appreciation
to the individuals, organizations, and publishers
who granted permission to quote their materials.
A list of acknowledgments is given on pages 125-27.

The Pilgrim Press
287 Park Avenue South, New York, New York 10010

Contents

Foreword

THIS IS A BOOK about death written for the living. The
reader will find its message direct, a celebration of the joy of
life, and an acceptance of the naturalness of death, without
knowing anything more about its author than she chose to
share. She wrote openly about her own early terror of death,
her inconsolable grief after she lost both her parents in the
first year of her marriage, her tears when she anticipated the
time when she would "no longer laugh, read books, drink
coffee, talk with friends, care for my family."

Her own words tell the reader of my mother's fears and
joys. But they do not tell all. Intentionally, I am sure, she did
not share her immediate and most pressing reason for writing
this book. And, inevitably, she could not write of her own
actual death.

Josephine Benton wrote *A Door Ajar* in the early 1960s (first
published in 1965) after my father was partially disabled by a
blood clot, which revealed an eventually fatal circulatory disease. Although she dedicated the book to her husband, she did
not mention him directly in the final chapter, "Being Companioned," when she wrote of "how much simpler it is to
face death ourselves than to be the one left sorrowing." The
shadow of a coming loss was, however, clear to her when she
wrote those words. What she could not know then is that

5

largely by a supreme effort of will to care for his wife, my father would remain alive for almost fifteen years, and only when he had done all he could for her did he accept, with relief, the death he had avoided so long. Frederic Elmon Benton died June 17, 1977, and on that day my mother rallied from her own illness to pronounce his finest epitaph: "He was a good man."

Her own illness, yes—how did the author of *A Door Ajar* meet death herself? Did she walk through that door without fear?

I think I know the answer, for by an ironic twist of fate Josephine Benton stepped over the threshold toward death while she was still alive and could communicate with her loved ones, her husband, my sister, my wife and me and her grandchildren, her relatives and friends who visited her in the nursing home. A few years after she wrote this book, progressive atherosclerosis began to close off the supply of blood to her brain, destroying first her memory and then more and more of the functions of cerebral control. In the early stages of the disease she knew what was happening to her. "I was proud of my mind when I had one," she would say, and then, forgetting that she had just spoken, would say it again.

One of her favorite books was Thornton Wilder's *Our Town*, where the dead in the cemetery above Grovers Corners can look down on their beloved town, at first long to return, follow with interest the news of events large and small, and then slowly and surely become more distant from the life of this world, move into an acceptance of their own loving here and now and their place in eternity. This process my mother went through in her own last years, and those who were close to her could see how she faced her particular combination of life and death.

She was, I feel sure, without fear of death. But she did not go gentle into that good night. In the words of Dylan Thomas, she did "rage, rage against the dying of the light." She loved life too intensely not to struggle against her own deterioration and only locked doors could keep her from walking free. She did did not "learn to welcome death." She did accept it without fear.

Josephine Moffett Benton died on August 4, 1978, a month after her seventy-third birthday. On that birthday, although she could neither walk nor complete a sentence, she still actively expressed her elemental values, smiling with joy at the growth and pleasure of a child, greeting a stranger with dignity and interest, reaching out a hand to touch another in shared affection.

As this book shows, Josephine Benton found her inner strength in religion and in poetry. In another of her books she posed Thornton Wilder's question of whether any of us ever fully realize life while we live it. The answer could have been written of her: "Saints and poets maybe—they do *some.*"

JOHN FREDERIC BENTON

Preface

IN EVERY LIFE there are two elemental facts over which no one has a choice. I did not choose to be born into this world; neither can I refuse to die. And yet for years, at the back of my mind, the fear of death was an almost constant companion.

I remember a funeral where I wept unrestrainedly, not primarily for the loss of the dear old man we had come to honor, though of a certainty he would be missed. I wept for the me who would one day no longer laugh, read books, drink coffee, talk with friends, care for my family.

But an attitude toward death can change and does, though no one can simply grit his teeth and choose to feel a calm acceptance toward death as well as life. How one feels about life may contribute more than we know to how one feels about death. The person who gives thanks each morning for the new day with its opportunities to work, to learn, to serve, to worship, in all likelihood at night welcomes sleep and at the end has no fear of death.

That which is truly desired has a way of coming to pass. I thought about and sought after and longed for a new perspective. I cannot name the day when I consciously knew that death was no longer a dreaded terror. But I had listened and learned, read and searched, meditated and prayed. The time did arrive when with as much certainty as anyone has about an untried situation, I could hope that without fear

I myself might walk through—or I could see those I love enter—that door which forever stands ajar.

Even as perspective in an individual can change, so from generation to generation customs change. In times gone by the last words of the dying were collected and prized; ministers followed the instructions of the prayer book urging the person upon his deathbed to confess his sins and prepare to face his Maker. Abandoning such practices is no doubt a step forward, but is it not a leap into unreality to discard all mention of the possibility of death, to move about in a world of fantasy as if we would walk on the solid ground of earth forever?

In my mother's day a woman with child would not go out in public once her condition became obvious. Now the expectant mother is relaxed, takes her pregnancy for granted, carries her head high, dresses becomingly, and takes pride in her fruitfulness.

Changes have come to pass in this modern world not only in regard to pregnancy, but also to birth. Ideally childbirth is without fear and with consciousness of the process. The husband is often with his wife during labor and by her side at the moment of delivery. Mothers are on their feet almost immediately. And yet no longer than thirty years ago we pitied the Indian squaw and the Chinese peasants who dropped their babies and went back to work.

If so much good sense is being resurrected from the primitive past in regard to being born, perhaps some of the exaggerated restraint, the blanket of silence, the shroud of secrecy that encompasses dying can be lifted. Death is as natural, as much a part of life, as birth. Can we learn to welcome—or at least accept—death without fear even as young mothers face, with full consciousness, birth without fear?

JOSEPHINE MOFFETT BENTON

CHAPTER ONE

Healing Words

As a child I was terrified of death. The predestination-damnation sermons of my Hard-Shell Baptist uncles reminded us—young and old—that only the elect of God would be saved by grace from the everlasting fires of hell. And I dreaded the ordeal of funerals where the ordinarily jolly old aunts were transformed into heavily veiled widows, who seemed never to cease wiping their eyes on black-bordered linen handkerchiefs.

Even as a young wife I was still afraid of death. Hours were spent searching my memory and writing out lists of all the women I knew personally who had died in childbirth, or whose babies had been stillborn—tragedies far more common in the United States forty years ago than now.

In this first year of our marriage both my parents died—first my father, and six months later my mother. My grief was elemental and inconsolable. A product of the cynical and agnostic twenties, I could not find even a thin thread of faith to lift me from my selfish sorrow.

When our baby was eight months old we moved from Chicago to Philadelphia, where my husband's father was minister of the Universalist Church of the Messiah. Out of family loyalty we began to attend services. A practice which began as a duty became a privilege as I was touched by the inspired words of this good man.

In time I also came under the influence of Harry Emerson Fosdick. On a visit to Riverside Church I discovered his previous sermons, printed and on sale for ten cents each. What treasures were mine for a dollar! One of them was an Easter Sunday sermon preached on April 16, 1933 entitled "The Soul's Invincible Surmise."

Thanks to these two men, my faith increased and my fears of death fell away.

THE SOUL'S INVINCIBLE SURMISE

O world, thou choosest not the better part!
It is not wisdom to be only wise,
And on the inward vision close the eyes;
But it is wisdom to believe the heart.
Columbus found a world, and had no chart
Save one that faith deciphered in the skies;
To trust the soul's invincible surmise
Was all his science and his only art.
Our knowledge is a torch of smoky pine
That lights the pathway but one step ahead
Across a void of mystery and dread.
Bid, then, the tender light of faith to shine
By which alone the mortal heart is led
Unto the thinking of the thought divine.

—George Santayana

» Every one of us has an intimate, personal concern with the Easter message. We all have had family and friends who have gone down into the experience of death and have

---

» Long or independent prose quotations are set off with chevrons. « Sources and acknowledgments are listed on pages 125-27.

disappeared into the invisible. We ourselves face that same experience—we have a rendezvous with death—when we, too, shall disappear into the unseen. And facing this universal fact of death it is difficult, I think, for any man altogether to escape, at least at times, to use Santayana's phrase, "the soul's invincible surmise" about that unseen world. . . .

We approach the clarifying of that surmise by remarking that the real difficulty which most of us experience in holding a vital faith in immortality lies not so much in our intellects with their arguments as in our imagination. We cannot picture immortal life. . . . Our friends disappear, we say, into the invisible. . . . Seeing is believing we say, and then, out of this world of the seen our friends disappear into the unseen. No wonder that life beyond death is not real to us; we cannot picture it. . . .

There is, I suspect, only one answer to that: we must perceive that now, not after death alone but today, we really live in an invisible world. . . .

For one thing, we ourselves are invisible. Our bodies can be seen but not our personalities. Personality is self-conscious being with powers of intellect, purpose, and goodwill. We cannot see that. Self-conscious being, mind, purpose, love—their effects are visible and their embodiments our eyes can see but they themselves, the creative realities behind the visible, are invisible forever. . . .

What is the difference . . . between life and death? Today my friend is alive; tomorrow the physicians say that he is dead—what has happened? The visible is here. Something invisible is gone. Life itself is invisible. All the realest forces in the world are invisible. Everything that we can see is only a shadow cast by something that we cannot see. "The things which are seen are temporal; but the things which are not seen are eternal."

We are not simply our bodies. The visible is only the surface of us, and even here and now deep beyond deep lies behind that in the world invisible.

To be sure, everybody knows how natural it is to feel that life beyond death is too mysterious, too marvelous, too good, it may be, to be true. But, my friends, consider. The real mystery is not thus postmortem; the mystery is here and now. We are inhabitants today of the world invisible; that is the mystery. Sometimes when one ponders it, how everywhere the visible world is but a door which, when we push it open, ushers us into a world invisible, one bows in awe unspeakable. There is not a mystery about the unseen world beyond death that is not essentially here now.

Indeed this, I think, would be the mystery, that this universe should produce personality with its amazing possibilities of knowing, creating, loving—imprisoned splendors, such as exist in all the cosmos nowhere except in personality—and then, having produced the spiritual world invisible, should snuff it out like a guttering candle as though it did not matter. That would be a mystery. . . .

Countless questions about our friends who have disappeared into the unseen we cannot answer. We had better be agnostic about details. Only charlatans pretend to know them. This, however, is true, that when a soul who long has dwelt in the unseen disappears into the invisible it must be like going home. On that day, long ago when Jesus passed into the "house not made with hands, eternal, in the heavens," do you think it seemed strange to him? Had he not always lived in the unseen, from it drawn power, to it given his devotion, for it laid down his life? Was not disappearing into the unseen for him like going home? . . .

Go out, then, on this Easter day, with a song of triumph. The invisible is real. Say it to yourselves. Let it be a rallying cry to your souls when days are difficult and endurance hard, when death befalls your friends or, like a "dark mother always gliding near with soft feet," comes to your own door-sill. The invisible is real. Let it challenge your conscience also, when carnal things loom too vivid and spiritual values seem too dim. The invisible is real. Let it usher you now into life eternal so that when the great change comes it may be for you, whose real life long has been in the unseen, like going home. For this is the root of all great religion, this is the meaning of all faith in God, this is the basis of immortal hope, this is the radiance of the Easter morning, that we endure as seeing him who is—aye, and those who are—invisible.

Prayer: O God, we who deal so much with sight pray thee for the grace of insight, in the spirit of Christ. AMEN. «

—Harry Emerson Fosdick

HEALING WORDS

For most of us the loss of parents and older relations, friends, and neighbors, must be borne long before any thought of personal death is considered. How we talk to ourselves, the things we read, can be a means of finding solace.

Why is man given the gift of speech, why do we strive for worldwide literacy if such art does no more than inform the mind? The poems and brief meditations that follow may help to heal the broken heart. Of a certainty, pouring out their grief in words has been a means of alleviating the sorrow of the writers. This is true of the first poem which was written by an eighteen-year-old youth after witnessing the death of a friend by drowning.

A silent throng
of people stood
about a silent form
and bending willows
softly sang

a noiseless,
silent tune.
A blade of grass
bent underfoot
wailed out a
silent cry,
and silent birds
on silent wings
looked down
on one who died.
                              —James Reinke

But this we know: our loved and dead, if they should come
    this day—
Should come and ask us, "What is life?"—not one of us could
    say.
Life is a mystery, as deep as ever death can be;
Yet, oh, how dear it is to us, this life we live and see!

Then might they say—these vanished ones—and blessed is
    the thought,
"So death is sweet to us, beloved! though we may show you
    naught;
We may not to the quick reveal the mystery of death—
Ye cannot tell us, if ye would, the mystery of breath!"

The child who enters life comes not with knowledge or
    intent,
So those who enter death must go as little children sent.
Nothing is known. But I believe that God is overhead;
And as life is to the living, so death is to the dead.
                              —Mary Mapes Dodge

In times of joy and times of grief
These I have loved beyond belief,
These I have loved and always will:

All trees that grow, and every hill,
Fields newly plowed, young corn in rows,
The old dark prophecies of crows.
Evening wind in willow thickets,
Frog songs and the songs of crickets,
Stone walls that wear frail lichen lace,
The daisy's round and sun-washed face,
Lanes over which wild grasses lean,
All things my own hands have scrubbed clean.
These I have loved in times of pain
And times of happiness: the rain,
First stars, white moonlight; nor shall I
Leave them behind the day I die!

—Elizabeth-Ellen Long

Still, still with thee, when purple morning breaketh,
When the bird waketh and the shadows flee;
Fairer than morning, lovelier than the daylight,
Dawns the sweet consciousness, I am with thee!

Alone with thee, amid the mystic shadows,
The solemn hush of nature newly born;
Alone with thee, in breathless adoration,
In the calm dew and freshness of the morn.

When sinks the soul, subdued by toil, to slumber,
Its closing eyes look up to thee in prayer;
Sweet the repose beneath thy wings o'ershading,
But sweeter still to wake and find thee there.

So shall it be at last, in that bright morning,
When the soul waketh and life's shadows flee;
Oh, in that hour, fairer than daylight dawning,
Shall rise the glorious thought, I am with thee!

—Harriet Beecher Stowe

Marylu Terral Jeans sent me her poem "Home for Christmas," explaining, "This one is for my father and all loved ones who die during the Christmas season."

> Not yet—not yet! we cry, but who can say
> What hour the leaf shall fall, the moon shall wane?
> The Christmas tree is fragrant and aglow,
> But Christmas will not be the same again.
> No more the scent of evergreen will mark
> This season for me, as it has before.
> I catch the scent of flowers in the dark;
> I hear the organ sound, the closing door . . .
>
> But one who loves and is loved never dies;
> He lives forever in the mind and heart,
> And who can say how high the spirit flies
> When life's cocoon allows it to depart?
> This much I know: The one we love is free,
> And Home for Christmas, as he wished to be.

In the seventeenth century Jeremy Taylor spoke these words of comfort: "When a good man dies, one that hath lived innocently, . . . then the joys break forth through the clouds of sickness, and the conscience stands upright, and confesses the glories of God, and owns so much integrity that it can hope for pardon and obtain it too. Then the sorrows of sickness . . . do but untie the soul from its chain and let it go forth, first into liberty and then into glory."

» All who have meant good work with their whole hearts, have done good work, although they may die before they have the time to sign it. Every heart that has beat strong and cheerfully has left a hopeful impulse behind it in the world, and bettered the tradition of mankind. «

—Robert Louis Stevenson

» For dear and lovely souls who have been our companions and from whose strong and kindly living we have been kindled with an inner flame, we thank thee. We gather up into our prayer today the far-flung fellowship of those we love, though death has parted us or distance separate us now. Make us one in the unity of a spiritual companionship stronger than distance and more enduring than death. AMEN. «

—Harry Emerson Fosdick

» Christ binds us all together and reveals us one to another. All that my mouth cannot make my brother and sister understand, he will tell them better than I can ever do. All that my heart desires for them, with an anxious and powerless ardor, he will bestow upon them, if it is good. All that others fail to hear from my feeble voice, all that they close their eyes to avoid hearing I have the resource of confiding to Christ who will repeat it in their hearts. And if this be so, I can die with my ideal, be buried with the vision I longed to share with others. Because Christ gathers up for the life to come, if they are sincere, all my unfulfilled ambitions, my partial insights, all my blunderings and unfinished efforts.

So, Lord, now lettest thou thy servant depart in peace. «

—Pierre Teilhard de Chardin

A LITANY FOR THOSE WHO MOURN

» Father of all mercy, we commit to thy loving care our dear ones, departed out of this world, and beseech thee to give us understanding and courageous hearts.

Loose us from the bitterness that casts a shadow over all the common day, that we may gain the peace which comes from ceasing to protest,

We beseech thee, good Lord.
For the years of fulfillment, for the joys we have known, and for the glad memories that crowd our hearts,
We thank thee, good Lord.
For the daily tasks which fill our empty hands, for habit born of years of training, which holds us steady in the storm,
We thank thee, good Lord.
For the unexpected tribute, and the revealing of new beauty in those we have known before; for eager hands held out to help us in our dire need, and for the understanding service of our friends,
We thank thee, good Lord.
For tears freely shed which heal and bring release, and which in thine own good time thou wilt wipe away,
We thank thee, good Lord.
For the strength, born of our own travail, to help others new in sorrow; for that rare insight vouchsafed [to] us, which is the gift of grief,
We thank thee, good Lord.
For the ever-present wounds of the spirit, which in God's mercy bring us near to him, and by their very perpetuity prevent our leaving him,
We thank thee, good Lord.
For the gradual but sure transformation of our physical loss into spiritual gain as the years go by,
We thank thee, good Lord.
For the courage which bids us carry on in new adventure, confident of the nearness and understanding of those we have lost,
We thank thee, good Lord.
For all those who share our precious memories, who knew and loved our dear ones and who now help to keep their memory clear,
We give thee special thanks, good Lord.

Above all for the hope thou hast given us through thy blessed Son Jesus Christ, of life eternal in the company of our loved ones,
We give thee grateful hearts, good Lord.
We thy servants who have passed through the valley of the shadow of death, fear no evil. Sanctify us through our grief, that we may know the close communion of the saints, and lift our lives to theirs, and so live fully through the years. In the name of him who was the firstfruits of them that sleep, Jesus Christ our Lord. AMEN. «

ENGLISH EASTER

The solemn fields breathe out to me
    A homely magic and austere:
The wonder and the sanctity
    Of shrouded life, is here.

On such a morning grey and still
    I think it was, that Mary went
By such a path below the hill,
    On love's last errand bent.

She saw the coppice rosy-brown,
    She saw the catkin on the bough,
And Calvary as yonder down
    That stands above the plough.

Sweet in the sleepy morn it stood,
    White on its slopes the cropping sheep;
Dark in its folds the little wood
    Where Life was laid to sleep.

Oh, sought she there, as I, in vain
    Place for her tears, her heaviness:
To find, where Perfect Love was lain,
    Upspringing loveliness?

And had he touched to sudden bloom
  The platted blackthorn at the door?
Enveiled with budding life his tomb,
  Made violet-blue the floor?

Did Mary stand, as I today
  Encompassed by that life newborn;
And see his sigil on the spray,
  His sign amidst the thorn?

And know the cruel winter done,
  And know the spring was come indeed—
Soft-stepping in the wake of One
  Whose feet were on the mead?

O shining buds upon the pine!
  O pulsing sap within the tree!
Behold the endless clue is mine
  Which leads where I would be.
                        —Evelyn Underhill

PRAY AND REST

Alan Paton is one of our greatest living novelists. It is more than the beauty of his style, more than the gripping story he tells, it is the point of view from which he writes. "If you asked me what kind of topics appealed to me in writing, I would have to confess to you that I couldn't bring myself to write any book which would increase the amount of depression and dejection that exists in so many people already. . . . [It's] a different thing where writing tragedy brings out a catharsis. My objection isn't to tragedy, because I believe tragedy and human life are inseparable. I believe that human life is meaningful and purposeful. . . . I should like to write books about South Africa which would really stab people in the conscience."

In *Cry, the Beloved Country* after Kumalo's son kills the white man, Father Vincent counsels and comforts the old preacher.

» —My friend, your anxiety turned to fear, and your fear turned to sorrow. But sorrow is better than fear. For fear impoverishes always, while sorrow may enrich. . . .

—It seems that God has turned from me, he said.

—That may seem to happen, said Father Vincent. But it does not happen, never, never, does it happen. . . .

When Kumalo had sat down, Father Vincent said to him, yes, I said pray and rest. Even if it is only words that you pray, and even if your resting is only lying on a bed. And do not pray for yourself, and do not pray to understand the ways of God. For they are secret. Who knows what life is, for life is a secret. And why you have compassion for a girl, when you yourself find no compassion, that is a secret. And why you go on, when it would seem better to die, that is a secret. Do not pray and think about these things now, there will be other times. Pray for Gertrude, and for her child, and for the girl that is to be your son's wife, and for the child that will be your grandchild. Pray for your wife and all at Ndotsheni. Pray for the woman and the children that are bereaved. Pray for the soul of him who was killed. Pray for us at the Mission House. . . . Pray for your own rebuilding. Pray for all white people, those who do justice, and those who would do justice if they were not afraid. And do not fear to pray for your son, and for his amendment.

—I hear you, said Kumalo humbly.

—And give thanks where you can give thanks. For nothing is better. Is there not your wife, and Mrs. Lithebe, and Msimangu, and this young white man at the reformatory? Now, for your son and his amendment, you will leave this to me and Msimangu; for you are too distraught to see God's will. And now, my son, go and pray, go and rest.

He helped the old man to his feet, and gave him his hat. And when Kumalo would have thanked him, he said, we do what is in us, and why it is in us, that is also a secret. It is Christ in us, crying that men may be succored and forgiven, even when he himself is forsaken. . . .

Kumalo looked at him under the light of the lamp. I believe, he said, but I have learned that it is a secret. Pain and suffering, they are a secret. Kindness and love, they are a secret. But I have learned that kindness and love can pay for pain and suffering. There is my wife, and you, my friend, and these people who welcomed me, and the child who is so eager to be with us here . . . so in my suffering I can believe.

—I have never thought that a Christian would be free of suffering, umfundisi. For our Lord suffered. And I come to believe that he suffered, not to save us from suffering, but to teach us how to bear suffering. For he knew that there is no life without suffering. «

—Alan Paton

CHAPTER TWO

Time to Die

BRADFORD SMITH, author of *Meditation: The Inward Art* and other books, was told that he had but a limited time to live. In all probability he had made his decision to "turn and live life to the hilt" long before the doctor gave him warning. For him life at its best included the setting down of his thoughts on paper. "The Road to Maturity" is but one of the meditations he wrote during his last months.

THE ROAD TO MATURITY

» One of the best-known legends of Buddha tells how his father kept him within the family park so that he would never know illness, old age, or death. But finally Buddha prevailed upon his charioteer to drive him three times beyond the gates. The first time he saw a man stricken with illness, the second time a man bent and wrinkled with age, and the third time a corpse.

"Must this happen even to me?" he asked. His charioteer assured him that it must.

So, with the knowledge that he too must die, Buddha began his long search for the way of life that would best cope with man's destiny. The point of the story is that no one has reached maturity until he has learned to face the fact of his own death and shaped his way of living accordingly.

Then the true perspective emerges. The preoccupation with material things, with accumulating goods or fame or power, is exposed. Then each morning seems new and fresh, as indeed it is. Every flower, every leaf, every greeting from a friend, every letter from a distance, every poem, and every song strikes with double impact, as if we were sensing it for the first and for the last time.

Once we accept the fact that we shall disappear, we also discover the larger self which relates us to our family and friends, to our neighborhood and community, to nation and humanity, and, indeed, to the whole creation out of which we have sprung. We are a part of all this, too, and death cannot entirely withdraw us from it. To the extent that we have poured ourselves into all these related groups and persons, we live on in them.

This relatedness of all life, as it binds us to all that has passed, surely binds us to the future as well. So the divine spark kindled in us can never really be extinguished, for it is part of a universal flame.

Once we have squarely faced the inescapable fact of our own death, we need never fear it, but turn and live life to the hilt. . . . Then, whether that life be long or short it will have been a full one. «

While fear of death may fade away with maturity and especially with a vibrant Christian faith, the thought of one's own personal dying may have been merely shelved as an abstract concept and banished behind the concerns of the day into a far distant future.

But it is an idea that should be taken down occasionally, dusted off, and considered with care. We may not have as many months to set our houses in order as did Hazel Andre and Lucile Fray. I am grateful for the courage and serenity of these two women. Because of their shining examples many of us will be more likely to make a good end.

Hazel Andre, wife of Floyd Andre, dean of agriculture at Iowa State College, wrote "My Last Best Days on Earth" in the last few weeks of her life. She explained that her experience "might help someone else face such a crisis."

MY LAST BEST DAYS ON EARTH

» If anyone had told me that the verdict "incurable cancer" would leave a trace of happiness for me, I would not have believed it. Because of this—and because death comes to every family—I am writing my experiences of these last days, when my life is in sharp focus. For I am one of the lucky ones who are granted the opportunity to prepare for death.

A year ago last September I was busy trying to "serve my turn" for each of my three children. I jumped hurdles to make committee meetings, to serve Sunday night supper to thirty members of the senior high youth fellowship group. In the midst of this, I came down with what we thought was flu. Like any mother, I stayed on my feet to help with a boy-girl campfire party, so important to my teen-agers. But by that time I knew I didn't have flu. Hepatitis, we thought next. After several months the doctors recommended exploratory surgery and I had it.

The report was probable cancer of the pancreas, but it couldn't be definite. So for a year we lived under a cloud that might not prove a certainty.

But what a wonderful year it was! Maybe because my husband and I knew there was a chance I wouldn't be around, life became more precious. We crowded in extras, things we might otherwise have postponed: two glorious weeks of camping, hiking, and fishing in the Grand Tetons. A family dream—having a farm near Ames, Iowa—came true. And we bought a riding horse.

This was our year of preparation. Even though we didn't talk about the possibility of my illness recurring, deep down my faith was being bolstered with the kind of miraculous strength that comes from outside ourselves when we need it. My mind and heart were watchful. I would catch a special meaning in a sentence. Like the statement at a women's meeting that a homemaker's efforts should be measured in the moments of happiness that she gives her family. Something impelled me to slip away early from this meeting so that I could join my husband who was going out to the farm.

Then last fall I went back to the hospital for the surgery which I knew would give the verdict. When it was over, my private nurse and friend whispered, "I wish there were some magic word I could say."

Then and there I ruled out bitterness and resentment. None of this "Why should it be I?" Why *shouldn't* it? Cancer kills indiscriminately. The hardest part about accepting death philosophically was the awareness that I was walking out on my husband and on three teen-agers at what seemed to me a time when a mother's counsel was a daily need. Tears dampened my pillow when I wrestled with that one.

Then my minister came with a book for me—*A Diary of Private Prayer* by John Baillie. God must have guided me quickly to these words, for they were the answer to my concern for my family: "I am content to leave all my dear ones to thy care, believing that thy love for them is greater than my own."

I asked my minister to mark passages in my Bible that would be particularly helpful in preparing me for death. These are the passages . . . John 14:1-3, 18-20; 16:16-23, 25, 33; and all of chapters 20 and 21; Romans 8:35-39; I Corinthians 15:35-44, 54-58; 2 Corinthians 5:1; Philippians 1:20-23; 1 Thessalonians 5:1-11; Revelation 21:1-4.

The next big step was to rule out all wish thoughts for the future. Family plans, personal projects, my dreams—I just forgot about them. For I knew that my happiness and serenity and that of my family would rest on the fact that I simply live for each day.

The day before Christmas I came home from the hospital. For ten weeks now, I have looked death in the eye, and I can truthfully say that each day has been gay, filled with peace of mind and overflowing with thankfulness for the thoughtful things done by friends and family.

Just as I had all the breaks for real happiness during my forty-two years of living, so am I still having the breaks! Drugs have relieved nausea and stopped much of the pain. How different if I were lying racked with pain and had to see my family struggling to take care of me. A housekeeper has come in and this leaves me free to enjoy my family and friends. (She will stay with my family when I am gone.)

The children know, of course. I told Alice and Richard, the two youngest. My husband always had been closer to our oldest daughter, Jackie, so he told her. . . .

There is a temptation, when time is running out, to crowd advice and admonitions into the last moments. That temptation I will not yield to. Through the years I've repeated my pet philosophies and I'm sure they're now a part of the children's code of living if they're ever going to be. . . .

In these past few weeks our home has been "open house" with a full pot of coffee and a sampling of food brought in by friends. When these friends drop in, it's their experiences I want to hear. By listening, my own life stretches out and I no longer feel bound by space or time.

One friend comes in each week and shampoos and sets my hair; a registered nurse stops in to give me a back rub.

Another friend helped my daughter cut out a dress for a special occasion. A friend who plays the piano beautifully drops in to give me music. On Sunday my friend's voice teacher is coming to sing "The Lord's Prayer," a favorite of mine.

I have the time to savor this daily richness. The hyacinth someone has grown especially for me, which I might have smelled so carelessly before, smells twice as fragrant.

I have no regrets—my life has been rich and full; I have loved every minute of it. But if I were to live it over, I would take more time for the savoring of beauty—sunrises; opening crab apple blossoms; the patina of an old brass coffeepot; the delighted surprised look on a tiny girl's face as she pets a kitty for the first time.

I would eliminate enough outside activities so that I could be always the serene core of my home—for the triumph of serenity has crystallized for me and my family in these last days.

I would get closer to people faster. When death is imminent we open our hearts quickly and wide. How much more Christian love there would be if we didn't wait for death to release our reserves!

I would live each day as if it were my last one, as I am doing now. «

A MOTHER'S LAST YEAR

» A young mother named Lucile Fray, knowing that she was desperately ill, decided to spend the last months of her life giving her ten children away. Many who heard about it pitied her. Some condemned her. Others wondered how she dared to take the terrible responsibility. She died on June 15, 1954, without really knowing whether she had done right or wrong.

This woman was not able to leave her children one penny's worth of material security. Yet she bequeathed to them the richest heritage a mother can hope to give.

Lucile McFarland Fray, a resident of Ottumwa, Iowa, had been married twelve years and was thirty-three years old when her tenth child was born. She named him Stephen. While she was in the hospital, she noticed a small lump on her left breast. She neglected to report it to her doctor.

"It's just a skin irritation," she told her husband, Ivan. "It'll clear up when I get home!"

Home, to Mrs. Fray, was a small rented three-room cottage. Five days later she was back there, cooking and caring for the baby, her nine other children, and her husband, a skilled foundry worker who had been all but crippled by arthritis several years before. She was busy, and for a while she forgot about the little reddening sore on her breast.

Mrs. Fray's neighbors say she was an excellent cook and seamstress, but not much of a housekeeper—not the scrubbing kind, anyway. "What's the use?" she used to say. "The kids follow along . . . and mess things up as fast as I clean!"

In the evenings Mrs. Fray liked to gather her youngsters around her in a circle and play a hilarious game of Old Maid or Slapjack. She was naturally musical and had a wide repertoire of folk songs that she had learned from her mother. She could play the mandolin and the guitar. She taught Joann, the eldest, to play the accordion. Six-year-old Frank, although subject to what appeared to be epileptic seizures, had a fine boy soprano. Joann recalls, "Some nights after supper, Dad grabbed up the guitar, Mom tuned up the mandolin, I got the accordion going, and all the rest of the kids sang along. Boy, what we used to do with 'San Antonio Rose'!"

Ten months after baby Stephen's birth, Mrs. Fray had an advanced malignant cancer. The breast was removed.

She returned home feeling well and cheerful. She sewed new dresses for the five girls, and she and her husband took the older boys on a hunting trip. Carl, the oldest boy, said admiringly, "Mom could sure handle a gun. She was a dead shot."

During the next year, the struggle to live at the Frays' became acute. Mr. Fray, with a serious case of arthritis, spent weeks in bed. Their savings vanished. In the spring Mrs. Fray went to the doctor again. This time the surgeons told her she had only months to live—perhaps a year.

In April she and her husband began to talk about the thing that worried them most. What would become of the children? Mr. Fray was now almost invalided. He had no immediate relatives. Mrs. Fray's mother, grandmother, and aunt were in no position either to support or to rear a brood of ten.

"One night I was giving Stephen a bath in the kitchen tub," Mrs. Fray later told the Rev. H. E. Goldboro of nearby Free Methodist Church. "I was turning the problem over in my mind. I couldn't bear to think of my children living in an orphanage. Suddenly I got a feeling that there was some kind of wonderful presence standing right beside me. I seemed to see a shining light. I said, 'Jesus has come to tell me what to do.' There were enough good people in the world to provide homes—good, loving homes—for all my children. I had to find them myself, before it was too late."

Although she often read to her children from the Bible, Lucile Fray was not a deeply religious woman. Until the last year of her life she was not a regular churchgoer. But to the end of her days she was convinced that on that night, in her extremity, she received divine guidance.

Ivan Fray agreed with great reluctance to his wife's plan to offer their children for adoption. "I told Lucile that, if I could get well and go back to full-time work, I might be able to keep them together," he said. "But she pointed out that the big burden would fall on Joann. She'd have to do all the mothering. She's a wonderful girl and she'd have done it willingly. But we thought she deserved a chance to have a life of her own. The same thing would have happened to Carl, our oldest boy. We wanted him to have an education and to be able to make something of himself."

In the next few weeks Mrs. Fray took each child aside and related, as simply as possible, what was going to happen. "We are all going to have new homes," was the way she put it to Linda, then not quite five years old. "I can't take care of you anymore because I am going to heaven to be with Jesus. But I'm going to find you another mommy who will love you just as much as I do!"

Word spread quickly that there were ten bright, fair-haired, handsome children available for adoption. When a small story appeared in the local newspaper, many couples came to knock at the Frays' door. But Mr. and Mrs. Fray weren't giving their children away to just anybody. Mrs. Fray had already drawn up a list of rather formidable checkpoints. They were:

1. Will you help the child to keep in touch with his brothers and sisters?
2. Does the adoptive father earn a steady living?
3. Are you happily married?
4. Do you believe in education?
5. Do you go to church?
6. Does your home have some modern conveniences?

Mrs. Fray, a woman who had known hard times, laughed at herself over this last requirement but clung stubbornly to it. "Indoor plumbing and electricity aren't really necessities to a child," she sighed. "But they do make the whole family's life easier. If you spend your time pumping water and cleaning lamps, you don't have time for much else."

Couples who seemed qualified and made a friendly approach to the child in whom they were interested were permitted to take him—or her—home for a few days' visit. When they returned, Mrs. Fray asked the child how he would like to have them as his new mommy and daddy.

"I know it wasn't very reliable, but I just had to take my child's word for it," she explained. "Sometimes there were couples that seemed to have every ideal requirement. I suppose a social agency wouldn't have hesitated—but I was the mother. Besides, I think children have an instinct about these things. Once Warren, my three-year-old, said he didn't want to go to live with one woman because she wouldn't let him holler. 'Not even a teeny bit!' he said. Well, I think he was right. Kids need to holler some!"

As Mrs. Fray had feared, the little ones were in greatest demand. Baby Stephen was the first to go. "We didn't believe it was true until we said good-bye to Stevie," Joann Fray told us. "Then we all got a little scared. Nobody cried, though. Instead we formed a family council to see what we could do to help Mother and make her feel happier."

The council decided to take over most of the household chores. "We knew Mom wanted to be able to spend her time with us," Pauline, eleven, explained. "Mom was artistic. She spent hours drawing and painting with the little ones. And she went hiking and hunting and berry-picking with the rest of us. I guess she was in pain, but she never let us know it." The family council voted to save their carfare money and buy their mother a present. They bought her a vase.

Alfred and Clara Johnson who own a middle-sized farm heard of the Frays' plight. The Johnsons have helped to rear more than a dozen foster children, but wanted one of their own. They had a hard time making up their minds which one to take. All the children looked attractive and presentable. All but Pauline, who was in bed with chicken pox.

"We decided that we wanted Pauline," Mrs. Johnson said. "I couldn't forget the sight of her lying there, all spotted up, but being cheerful and polite in spite of it!"

Joann, Virginia, Carl, Ivan Jr., Warren, and Frank were still waiting for a home. Mrs. Fray, now seriously ill and in constant pain, refused to lower her standards. A wealthy farmer and his wife were turned down because they said that education wasn't important. Another couple was also sent away. "They wanted to take Warren," Mrs. Fray told the family council, "but they wanted to cut all his ties with the past. Don't you worry, you'll all get good homes!" Only for six-year-old Frank was Lucile Fray resigned to the idea of institutional care. "They tell me Frank is an epileptic. It's no use my explaining what a darling he is. No one is going to take on a burden like that."

In December officials of the American Cancer Society entered the case. Mrs. Lucile Anderson, Iowa's senior field director, with the aid of the welfare department, found another, more suitable house for the Frays. A Christmas appeal brought food, clothing, toys, and some temporary financial support.

Mrs. Anderson and Mrs. Fray became good friends. "I've never met a more wonderful woman," Mrs. Anderson told us. "Right up to the end she kept up her spirit and great sense of humor. One day Frank decided to dye his hair. Somewhere he found a big bucket of green paint and dipped his head into it. When Mrs. Fray saw him she let out a shriek. Then she sat down and laughed and laughed. It took her hours to get the paint out, but she never got angry. She said to him, 'I ought to let you save it until St. Patrick's Day!'"

Mrs. Anderson wrote a moving letter to her sister. A few days later the Thomases were on their way to Ottumwa. When they arrived, they asked to meet all the children but only Joann was home. They sat down and drank tea. The

Thomases told Mrs. Fray about their church activities and about their house, which is situated on the edge of a lovely lake. "Before we went home, we knew we wanted Joann. She was a lovable girl. If we'd been fortunate enough to have a child of our own, she'd have been about that old."

Living for years on the edge of hardship, Joann is today a typical teen-ager. She has her own room; she swims, ice-skates, and roller-skates. Although she lost a year of schooling because of her mother's illness, she stands at the top of her sophomore class in high school. She attends church and Sunday school and sings in the choir.

The Thomases were so pleased with their good fortune that they set themselves the task of finding homes for the remaining Fray children. Within a week Virginia, Carl, and Ivan Jr., had found good homes. . . .

A few days later a young school superintendent and his wife, a school teacher, decided to adopt Warren Fray. Mrs. Fray stood dry-eyed in the door of her home as she watched the last of her adoptable children leave her forever.

The following week Mrs. Fray placed Frank in a hospital for physically incapacitated children. She lived near the institution for a week, visiting Frank every day, trying to ease the separation.

In the last spring an enlarging tumor broke one of Mrs. Fray's ribs. She was now in severe pain nearly all the time and realized that her death was very near. She was suddenly overwhelmed with the feeling she would like to see her children once more. Her doctor and husband protested, but she packed a small suitcase and boarded a bus.

At the nine homes, Mrs. Fray seemed to find everything satisfactory. She left a list with Joann, detailing the names, birth dates, and adoptive parents of all the other children. "If one of them is ever cut off from the rest of you," she said, "you'll be able to trace him."

Five days before her death, Lucile Fray entered a nursing home. She asked for and received baptism. "My house is in order," she told the Rev. Mr. Goldsboro. At the funeral the children looked steadily at their mother's face, then turned to their new parents for comfort.

In the summer the couple who had adopted Warren went to California to live. When they returned to pack up their furniture, they took him on a round of farewell visits. They took him to the children's hospital and he said good-bye to Frank. Frank asked, "Why don't I have a new mommy?"

No one answered him. "When we got home," Warren's father said, "neither my wife nor I could eat dinner. We just sat at the table, not saying anything, but each thinking the same thing. Then I said, 'It's an awful shame. He's such a handsome little boy!' And she said slowly, 'Epilepsy is some kind of brain injury, isn't it? It could happen to anybody! If we had a child of our own—who could say he'd be perfect?'"

When the couple and Warren moved to California, they took Frank with them. He, too, is now their legally adopted child. His seizures are increasingly rare and milder. Doctors there say he was probably never a real epileptic. They hold out hope of full recovery. The good news has traveled back to Iowa. «

AND A TIME TO DIE

And a Time to Die is the story of Mark Pelgrin who knew at the age of forty-seven he had incurable cancer. His personal sketches, journal, and poems were edited by two people who knew him and his family well, Jungian analysts Sheila Moon and Elizabeth B. Howes. They explained that Mark Pelgrin's "copious scrawled notes . . . delineate his personal journey, most particularly the culmination of that journey. We have felt this to be of great relevance for many people, because when a man thus faces his 'time to die,' he carries in his heart a universal confrontation and becomes an unintentional spokesman for all his brothers."

» The summer walks fast and July becomes August, the body restores and heals. I watch while with delight this fellow shuffles into his old clothes, takes the clippers and prunes the garden hedge or, . . . he makes a romp with the children, . . . or the getting of a meal, or the reading of a book, or when the feelings change, the despair when he is suddenly confronted with the future. And I feel like saying to him, "All right, fellow, you have had a strange life, all mortals have strange lives and I feel with you and this I'll admit is the strangest experience of all. Now what meaning do you make of it? Can you find the why in it?" And I weep for him and he weeps for me and we weep together. Jesus wept, we can weep, can't we? . . .

I have been afraid of crying, in the past, and have not allowed myself to feel instinctually, directly, as a man should. Crying is not a sissy act. It is a manly act, a recognition of what is deeply masculine in oneself. Too often I have not cried when I should have cried, or not laughed when I should have laughed. . . .

I had at last sensed the deep center of our humankind. It lies in love, but love that is direct and spontaneous and outgoing, and love that breaks down walls and thaws the chill of the mask, and love that blends the ego and the self, love not as a sentimental greeting card but as a point of tension, a unity of opposites in which dislike attracts like and like attracts dislike and all strange beasts lie down together where the newborn child is. It is love of this kind, passionate yet dispassionate love, that leads a man to accomplish what

Laotze says when he asks, "Can your learned head take leaven from the wisdom of your heart?". . .

How much purpose or meaning can we find in what we do? If we are free agents, given freedom by God, then we can learn the way of sacrifice, of "making holy," yielding up, for spiritual growth. But what about cancer, or accidents that come meaninglessly and cut us off, break us down, not at the end but in the clear middle of life? What about the earthquake, the hurricane, the insidious hurricane within that is the incurable disease? What about that? . . .

So I would be in a delightful present moment, playing anagrams with John and talking with Eric at the same time and watching Ruth play with the girls, all dressed up in their Sunday dresses, and the fire burning in the fireplace, and that moment would break and I would start worrying, "What about them? How can they do without me?" And then I would force myself back to the present. The fullness of this day, this Now, is a certainty that I can be anchored to. I cannot control or order the destiny of these children, I cannot, living or dead, know what they will be or how they will grow. But if I live fully now this can be the greatest gift I can make to them. The more I am compulsive in my intuitive anxiety about them the less I can give them. I can trust my love, love now. What more do I need for fullness? . . .

"Ye shall enter the kingdom of heaven as a little child." Now what did he mean by that? Not the same as a little child. But with still some of the child's awe, his sense of wonder, perhaps? And was the difference reverence? . . .

Consider my attitude to the boys when they were tiny and the girls now they are tiny. Then I was always too busy and anxious about my vast intuitive plans to enjoy them at all. Saturday meant Saturday not with them in sandplay, as it could have been, but Saturday in the library taking notes from tomes that would supposedly be distilled into a great book—which I never did finally complete. . . . Now my attitude . . . is all in search of personal meaning, not big philosophic meaning, but the kind of personal meaning that comes with sticking a candle in a child's birthday cake or making a soup. Meaning, or so I discovered yesterday, can be found when a child puts daddy's hat on her head and laughs with that spontaneous crackle a girl can burst into when she has half a joke to it. . . .

The cancer patient is put on a year-to-year basis. . . . Well, what does one do? In one sense, one goes on the way one has always. A man with a job and family, as in my case, goes on with his job and supports his family and enjoys his family and helps around the house, as always. But there is a little extra ceremony to it. This might be the last time I am teaching my favorite courses, so I am tempted to do my very best, and even allow myself luxuries in teaching I have not allowed before, . . . like getting to know my students better, trying to draw them out in class discussion uninterrupted by "the professor," and when I am called upon to interpret, trusting to my spontaneous "wisdom." I feel much more that I want to listen to life, to my colleagues and students, and to what the literature I am teaching really says, and to hold my opinions more in suspension.

Family life becomes more of a ceremony. I feel like spending more time with the children, playing with them, talking with them, listening to them. To say grace at meals. And silent prayers at the bedside at night. And particularly, at the end of the day, to ask and thank the Creator. To ask every day for my "daily bread," some spiritual refreshment, some insight for growth, some joy, something that makes each day stand out among the others. The facade of time is stripped away and every day now becomes a kind of journey.

How surprising life is, as though the future, as it impinges upon this moment, is laden with surprise, with treasures to be rescued from it!

And perhaps I can discover, in this onrushing future, new sides of myself, neglected sides of myself; perhaps I can be, as much as possible, all I have not been. For if there is any goal in our lives it is this: to pass beyond ourselves as we now are, to be open to change and creativity, to become more conscious, more integrated, more rounded, more complete; and this one can do by embracing, openhanded, each new challenge and each new possibility, rather than by rejecting them for a static self-satisfied adherence to what has long been established. . . .

Indeed, the reason for living now is not because time is short but because now is where life is. . . .

Epilogue: Outside the room the hospital world moved at its accustomed pace, with its usual sounds of ministration. Inside—what was really there? Did it consist of us who loved him? . . . Was it Mark Pelgrin himself, looking so intently and remotely into places we could not see? Whatever was there, whoever really came and went during that timeless day, and what emotions rose and fell with the hissing oxygen —who could say with certainty? It was clear only that death and life moved together.

Despite the equipment of medical science surrounding him, . . . Mark was a man, a man filled with dignity. He could not speak; no strength was available for that. But as I came to him, his hand grasped mine and his eyes smiled. "All shall be well and / All manner of thing shall be well." The words I said had been a sort of refrain for him during the past week, and he nodded, hearing them, and his lips formed them soundlessly. And those other words I had spoken a week before to tell him that the operation was useless and that

his life was over—those words, too, I repeated: "I said to my
soul, be still, and let the dark come upon you / Which shall
be the darkness of God." . . .

Three pictures had been with Mark for many days, and all
three were in the room—a copy of the compelling Rouault
painting "The Holy Face," the mysterious Chinese temple
painting, and a large photograph, done by a friend, of a
blossoming apple bough against a spring sky. More than once
Mark indicated with hand or eyes that he wanted one of
these brought closer; and when one of us held them where
Mark could see, he seemed to peer into and through them,
often nodding his head or moving his lips. Time and space
did not exist, so it seemed, but only being—and being was in
the center of a dark circle, or in the stark gaze of "The Holy
Face" meeting the stark gaze of the man on the bed, or in
the point of light at the ephemeral tip of an apple branch.
Occasionally I spoke to him softly of matters that I knew
concerned him. More often there was an indescribable
silence into which the world's noise came muted and alien.
Once he asked for a pencil and paper. Slowly and with great
effort he drew a circle and then a cross.

"Do you want a prayer?" I asked.

He nodded.

"Our Father which art in heaven . . ." The familiar-un-
familiar words closed about us, drew us into a place "beyond
hope and despair" and held us suspended in the mystery. At
the end of the prayer Mark whispered almost inaudibly,
"Everything is a circle." «

CHAPTER THREE

Death Came for a Child

LIVING WITH the knowledge of one's own sure and approaching death presents one valley to cross through. Watching a beloved child die must be the greatest grief of all—a tremendous range of mountains over which to climb.

One mother translated the experience into poetry. Mrs. Richardson writes that the last thing she heard Ann say a few hours before her death was: "Now I am going down the little path to show them all my new clothes."

> She lay upon her pillow,
> Small queen, at her levee,
> And entertained her Visitor
> With royal courtesy.
> She showed him all the treasures
> Which lay upon her bed,
> And of his stony visage
> She seemed no whit afraid.
> She sang to him a little song
> In fluttering voice and low,
> Then smiled at me and softly said,
> "I'm tired. May I go?"

Outside the spring wind tossed the trees
In sudden ecstasy.
The child had passed.
She left behind
Her Visitor with me.

—Margaret S. Richardson

The loss of a child seems to enable some mothers to stand on the threshold and to gain a glimpse of ultimate reality. A mother of five children writes of the death of her second daughter: "Perhaps you have heard that Marjie left us for a better existence. All in all, it has been an amazing and inspiring experience for us. She was such a remarkable child—gifted and rather mature in spiritual understanding—and we feel lucky to have had her. Now she is in a special category—always to be remembered young. She has given us a special strength and inspiration. We have felt so lifted up. I thought that meant she would get well, but it was somehow to be that her passing would set us in tune with spiritual reality. The whole experience has made us much more aware of the necessity of purifying our thoughts and actions, of living with God."

Catherine Gabrielson wrote a more detailed account of the death of a child in her book *The Story of Gabrielle.*

THE STORY OF GABRIELLE

» You were nine that summer—a long-legged, sun-kissed little girl with long, straight, sun-bleached hair. You were strong and healthy, full of lively, irrepressible spirits. You had abundant energy and an extraordinary capacity to savor each day as though it were your first or last.

On the weekend before school closed for the Christmas

holidays you got sick. One afternoon the pains began again and got steadily worse. You turned to me suddenly. "No one in the world will be able to cure me of this," you said, "and I will die of this pain."

One afternoon we were sitting quietly when you said, suddenly, "Oh, Mummy, I feel so funny, I feel so strange. It isn't physical. It's very important. I wonder what it means."

"Perhaps God has just given you some extra energy," I offered lamely, in explanation. When Daddy came from work a few minutes later, you told him happily that you had just had a wonderful experience—God had given you some energy.

Dr. Lynde ordered the operation for Saturday morning. You were upset and began to cry when we told you. I had to remind you that I expected you to be very brave, just as, later on, you had to remind me.

Our old friend Dave [a radiologist] came in. "We know of nothing we can do. We don't know how long Gabby can live. It may be a matter of weeks or months."

Even though the doctors said it was hopeless, Daddy and I were determined to try something. But what?

I made an appointment to see a cancer specialist. He gave me what turned out to be very good advice. He said firmly that you were in the best possible hospital, with the best possible doctors and that to travel around the country, or the world, trying to find something to help you would be futile, exhausting, nerve-racking, and unfair, besides being fabulously expensive.

It was hard for us to let go of the idea that somewhere, somehow, someone could do something. But we did stop searching in that way. Instead we substituted faith and began to live from day to day, knowing that each day might be the last for you, and therefore was a special day, full of significance, to be enjoyed completely.

You were always terribly good at living in the moment anyway, being twice as alive as most people.

You seemed quite determined not to surrender yourself completely to all the goings-on inside you. "After all, it's only the body," we would agree. The real Gabby was as well and alive as ever. Perhaps even more so.

Often [when I reentered your room], I would experience the exhilaration that comes with a heightened sense of life, not death. I was always conscious of the small miracle that you were still alive. I could touch you, kiss your forehead, tell my love. Besides, there was a special quality of light or lightness around you. Many things were painful, but the atmosphere was never gloomy.

One night late as we were preparing for bed, you said, quite unexpectedly, "You looked worried today." "And I don't like that," you said, almost sternly. "I expect you to be able to go through all these things without breaking down."

"Without breaking down," what a grown-up phrase! I felt as though a steady hand had been placed on my shoulder.

On [the] Saturday before Easter, I felt uneasy about you. "The call is coming, the call is coming," you sang out in a singsong way several times. You looked so very strange that, alarmed, I rang for the nurse. Just as she came to your bedside, you had your first convulsion.

"You had better step outside," the nurse said to me. Step outside? What an impossible request! I assured the nurse that I wasn't frightened by convulsions and that I had no intention of leaving you at such a crucial moment. Dawn came and you hadn't died.

On Tuesday your temperature gradually began to subside. You looked at us with a big smile. You looked around the room with interest as though you had been away on a long journey.

You were sleeping or dozing most of the time now. You

moved around in bed these days with great difficulty. "If you don't move around," I told you one afternoon, "you'll get as stiff as an old woman."

"I *am* an old woman." You smiled back. "I'm infinity years old."

Sometimes now I wonder whether I should have told you the verdict of the doctors. But I don't think it would have made any difference. Death is implied and understood in living, if you really live, and we were certainly deeply immersed in that in our way. I think you understood.

Friday, April 25, was a quiet day. Late that night, you added an afterthought to our good-night chat. "Sweet dreams," you whispered, and these were, without warning, your last words for me.

The doctors suggested that we should leave you and wait outside in the room for visitors. Think of it, the greatest event of your life, and they wanted us to wait outside. Daddy and I sat by your bed. He held his watch and I held your wrist, counting your pulse. Once in a while I bent over to kiss your forehead, and you always moved your lips in a kiss for me.

Your pulse slowed down to almost nothing. I looked at Daddy—and then we knew you weren't really there anymore.

We picked arbutus all morning on the day of your funeral. The shy, fragrant sprays were in hiding everywhere on the April hills. [We] picked in all your favorite spots. Together we wove a blanket of arbutus for your small white coffin. «

WE GIVE THANKS

When the death of a child follows even a brief illness, the time of waiting is a gift—time to hope, time to express love, time to face possible loss, time to pray for strength whatever comes, time to try to accept life and death as two parts of one whole.

The shock of sudden death by accident of a friend or member of the family poses a harder problem. But death by violence? However can parents come to terms with the murder of a beloved daughter? What words can be spoken that will set free the healing process?

"We are here to give thanks for the life of Janice Wylie." That sentence "meant something" to Max Wylie, the bereaved father who wrote about his daughter's tragic murder.

» The newspaper details of the loss of our daughter Janice, murdered with Emily Hoffert, . . . have been widely publicized. To those who know our small family here in New York, we seem to be taking the lash of this unspeakable horror without flinching. This is not so.

It is even possible that we will finally break up with grief, or be broken down by frustration: the frustration, perhaps, of never finding the killer; the frustration of a daylight double killing so wild and furious that the lack of a findable clue [and the lack of] a guessable motive combine maliciously, as if daring the mind to snap. Most of all, there is the smothering frustration of the senseless waste of so much goodness, so much love; the waste of all those thousands of hours that preoccupy the minds of parents everywhere; the pervasive, continuous, powerful sense of responsible protectiveness all parents feel toward their children, whatever their age. Janice was twenty-one. . . .

In trying to learn how to bear the unbearable, have we discovered resources of endurance not given to others? Have we secrets of adjustment, of special accommodation? Have we anything in our experience—joint or individual—or anything in our inheritances that we can describe for the direct benefit of others? to others who, loving their children, are crushed without warning under a catastrophe such as ours?

Surely no man, except in war, can prepare himself for the fact or the sight or even the possibility of such insane savagery as cut down our daughter Janice. At odd times, of course, such things are happening to other people. We hear about them. We read about them. On rare occasions—once or twice in a lifetime—something truly hideous overtakes someone we may know, or know of. But to *me*? To *my* family? . . .

It helped me—and I think it will help you if you need help —to get rid of all the rubbishy platitudes as soon as you can face the fact of your loss. God's hand is in none of these horrors. The most sustaining single sentence that came to us in over a thousand letters came from Janice's doctor: "This did not happen for the best; this happened for the worst." That was the truth of it. And that sentence, cold as it is, laid out the tragedy flat and bare and clean and final.

Another sentence comes back to me. And it is the theme of what I wish to relate. In its simplicity, the short sentence is unforgettable: "We are here to give thanks for the life of Janice Wylie." For the *life* of Janice Wylie! That meant something. And it came from a Presbyterian minister—the Rev. Dr. Paul Austin Wolfe.

We her parents, and our other daughter Pam, had had Janice—the excitement and exuberance of Janice, the fun and the fresh joy of her—for twenty-one years. . . . All the days of her twenty-one years, every one (and many of them troublesome) had been rich. That way, indeed, we were blessed. . . .

Because we Wylies, as children, saw so little of Father, vaguely fearing him, I kept my vow that were I to marry and have children, they would see me and know me and have fun with me. . . .

We took in the whole of it: ball games, Coney Island, ice

shows, symphonies, a zillion movies, musical comedies, zoos, the Central Park carrousel. No father has ever had a more exhilarating time with his daughters than I have had with Pam and Janice. . . .

Do the Wylies have "words to live by"? I think so, although none of us accepts God as the Christian churches urge us to accept him. . . . God had nothing to do with the murder of Janice, any more than he had anything to do with creating the hideous social deformity that is her killer. But the existence of a higher power seems to me to be necessary, not in the contemplation of the doings (the misdoings) of man-on-earth, but in the order of creation, and the unimaginable immensity of a universe in which the earth is a speck. . . .

The Wylies can't let down because Janice is dead. Others live, others who count on us, who need us. Others who loved Janice as we did. And many others whom we need. We must live the days as they come. . . . The heart bleeds, but does not break. Heartbreak is gratuitous wreckage. It is futility. In its way it is disloyalty too, not only to the one who is lost but to all those remaining who knew and loved. Heartbreak is for the weak and the hopeless and the half-alive. The whole purpose in living is in serving. Heartbreak *is* death.

So I say farewell, Janice, my darling. Thank you just for *being*. You were the larkish one: brave, merry, full of sun, full of song. You were vivid. You were loyal. Those who knew you . . . were lucky. . . . And it is your joy that has given us courage to be cheerful. Our remembrance is our gratitude; our gratitude, remembrance. . . .

"I come not to participate in hatred but to share in love."

Janice's ashes were scattered over the Adirondacks that she loved so—over its mountains and lakes. The words of Dr. Paul Wolfe keep coming back, freshening my family's spirit each time we think of them: "We come to give thanks for the life of Janice Wylie." «

CHAPTER FOUR

Dying Without Fear

I OFTEN THINK of that genuine faith of yours. . . . Because of this faith, I now remind you to stir up that inner fire which God gave you at your ordination. . . . For God has not given us a spirit of fear, but a spirit of power and love and a sound mind.   —2 Timothy 1:5-7 (PHILLIPS)

Between many happily married partners there exists a communication independent of words, a relationship based on understanding and community of interests. Sometimes, even for those so blessed, the desire to speak becomes a heartfelt need. For an old friend of ours the knowledge of her husband's incurable cancer proved to be an almost intolerable burden; she felt bound to keep silent because the truth of his condition was told only to her and not to him. Yet always before their troubles had been lightened, their joys increased, because they had borne them together.

Among other couples there are shining examples of husbands and wives who met death with greater equanimity because they could speak of their hopes and fears, their puzzlement at why this should happen to them, their joy and pain, their awareness of beauty in nature and human nature, the wonder of the now. Day after day for weeks, my neighbor has been going to the hospital to sit with her husband who is slowly slipping away because of a malignant tumor of the brain. And still this wife can write: "Tom is conscious and free of pain for which we are so thankful. Each day is precious and complete of itself. It is a quite wonderful experience in many ways."

THE HILLS OF HOME

Our doctor friend could diagnose the progress of the cancer that had metastasized throughout his body. One day he answered his wife's question, "How are you this morning?" with the familiar remark, "I must get worse before I can be better."

How well Mary understood his meaning. Often in the past when he was out late waiting to deliver a child he would call to report that hours must pass before he could start home. "This mother must get worse before she can get better," he would say. In birth and in death, there is apt to be a period of waiting, a time of labor, before the baby can be set free from the mother's body, the soul set free from the mortal body.

The knowledge that the cancer which had invaded his body would end Fred's life within six or eight weeks was harbored together by this man and woman who had shared their problems and pains, their successes and pleasures for more than thirty-five years. Together they decided he should spend his remaining days at home. Already he had endured two prolonged hospital stays—one for an operation and one for cobalt treatments. A practical nurse was engaged to stay with Fred in the mornings thus enabling Mary to keep her teaching position and to return with news of the outside world, amusing anecdotes, a fresh perspective. A rented hospital bed facilitated change of position for the patient and ease of care for those in attendance. Fred's doctor approved his having opium tablets on the bedside table where he himself could take them whenever the pain became unbearable. Neighbors stopped by to visit or run errands; one who was a nurse came every evening to help make Fred comfortable for the night.

And he had comfort, that is, fortitude for these last weeks. Though now residing in a city apartment, in an earlier chapter of their lives they had lived in an old farmhouse in Vermont. Their married son, still a Vermonter, saw no reason, nor did the attending doctor, why the father should not be taken by station wagon back to the hills of home. And so it came to pass that Dr. Fred spent his last two weeks in his son's home in the village where he had been a country doctor. He was cared for by his wife and children, and by his daughter-in-law, a trained nurse; in his good hours he enjoyed the presence of the grandchildren.

While the skill of a trained nurse was invaluable, Mary drew upon a fund of wisdom that perhaps only a doctor's wife could possess. She had heard again and again Fred's precise ideas of the care that should be given in a last illness: Never believe that because a patient is unconscious, or just dozing, he does not hear or at least sense what is said in his presence. Pray for him, reassure him that all will be well, speak often of your love. Of all the senses, hearing is generally the one which functions longest.

In those last days when the patient cannot tell you of his needs, try to imagine what will give him ease: change the position frequently, propping pillows under head and shoulders to facilitate breathing; give sponge baths and keep the bed dry and clean to prevent bedsores; massage legs and arms to lessen stiffness; keep the feet warm; give liquids frequently. If the patient is unconscious, moisten the inside of the mouth with water in which a few drops of lemon juice have been added.

Dr. Fred had a favorite story of an old wife who insisted her seemingly unconscious husband could communicate. The nurse saw no reason not to humor the old woman who was leaning over her spouse, speaking slowly and distinctly into his ear, "Would you like some hot tea?" No response. Undeterred by failure, she stood erect and said, "If you would enjoy a cup of tea, give me a signal." Immediately the patient waggled his finger to indicate yes.

Dr. Fred said, too, that there was no need to fear any struggle or agony at the end. The departure of the spirit from the physical body is as peaceful a process as a tired body falling asleep.

The day before his own death, Fred said to his wife, "I'll stay until tomorrow." And he did. On that last day, he said good-bye to each of his children, and to his wife a last grateful word of love. The story ends, as each of us might wish his life could end. After long years of service to humanity, and after tremendous growth in his own spiritual life, this man died in his son's home, in the green hills of Vermont he loved so dearly. His funeral was held in the small parish church where he and Mary had found their religious home.

My husband and I talked at length with Mary a few days later. Together we recalled episodes in Fred's life, instances of his kindness, his consideration, his humor. We remembered the times our paths had crossed and recrossed. Fred was in our thoughts, and we talked about him in a natural way.

It is a thing to learn that people in grief want above all else to speak of the one they mourn. They want to hear their friends pay tribute, or even just reminisce about common incidents or starred days in the life of the one now gone from sight and yet so vividly in their midst.

TESTAMENTS OF EXPERIENCE

Letters are one of the best expressions of true and spontaneous feeling. Firsthand experiences of wives who have met the death of a dearly beloved husband with "power and love and a sound mind" may prevent other women from "going to pieces." We do learn by example. Where there has been affectionate companionship, where there is no great guilt over things left undone or unsaid, thanksgiving for the years together can prevail.

» I want to share an experience I rarely discuss. My husband was an invalid for years. The last day before he died, he sat up in bed, with his eyes fixed on something he could see and I could not, and said, "I am late." Whatever he saw, wherever he was going, he approached it with joy. I know the pain and sorrow of going on alone without my dearest companion; yet I know he went to something better —free and unafraid—that is my joy. I tell you this so that sometime you may use it to comfort someone who needs it. «

» There are some few people to whom I feel I like to open my heart. And I want you to know that from the time of Ben's death I was reconciled to his going, felt it merciful he was released from burdens of a tired, frail body. As I sat by him in his last minutes it seemed to me God came and gently took him home; everything was so peaceful and quiet. I believe I have never been more conscious of the presence of God. However, I am not yet able to overcome the loneliness, the absence of a loved companion. «

» I do not usually look at a dead face if I can help it but L's was the most beautiful face I have ever seen, in the flesh or in marble or on canvas. Every minute of his eleven-year victory was in it. "Noble" was the word that flashed to my mind; then "victory"; then "the peace that passeth understanding." It was completely ageless. I know now what is meant by a spiritual body. «

» We returned home November 18th and were able to have [Bob] stay here until his death on December 22nd. There is no other explanation in my mind than that we were both "sustained by love." The Friends—and friends too—were wonderful in the messages they sent.

During the last days here at home, the family were also sustained by Sylvia Shaw Judson's *The Quiet Eye*. I'm sure you know it. "Be still and cool in thy own mind and spirit" and "Feeling light within, I walk" helped me most—but they were all divinely chosen, I feel.

Bob was so close to pure, disembodied spirit in his last weeks that it has given me a measure of peace. Yet it is hard to know that his spirit is still with me now—the perspective has changed. «

» Thank you for being our good friends. I am glad that you came to see us that last night at the hospital, for it helped make a pleasant evening for Ellsworth who, I am sure, did not have the "spirit of fear" but was confident. I know that now as always we are in God's hands. «

My friend, Lucille, knowing that her days were circumscribed, told me of her condition saying, "I thought you would want to know." She looked so serene, so beautiful, it didn't seem possible. Seeing the look of unbelief in my eyes she went on to say how important it was to her to wear pretty clothes, to look gay, especially for the sake of her husband. She said that long ago she had learned this art from her daughter. The little girl, speaking of an old neighbor, said, "Mama, isn't it nice that Belle Widener wears such frivolous, bright colors; she's always decked out in happy clothes, even on Sunday when she comes to Meeting."

Lucille had as little time for self-pity, for long faces, as did my friend, Mother Currier, who expressed her feelings in letters:

» AUGUST 7, 1949—In this mail will start your books. All three have given me enjoyment. On page 303 of *The Choice Is Always Ours* I've marked what is the finest thing there and copied it for my own help. So many people speak of the aged as weakening in all ways but Howard Collier stresses the strengthening of the spirit as the body fails. As when I came so near passing out of this life when operated on for a bad appendix, as the body weakened and even the voice went, I so strongly felt something within like a candle burning brightly each day.

"The growth-curve of the body rises by gradations from infancy until maturity; growth then remains stationary for a while and then, as bodily and mental decay begins to set in, the body-curve declines with increasing rapidity during middle life and old age. This decline is a healthy, normal state of affairs: death is no more pathological than birth. . . . The growth-line of the immortal spirit is very different. . . . As the one begins to decline, the other normally continues to rise and to develop. Increasing wisdom and ripening judgment are measures of this continuing spiritual growth. At last, as old age approaches, we can begin to observe how the 'free spirit' starts to loosen and detach itself from its bondage to the flesh, until at last the body returns to earth, and the spirit to God who gave it."

JUNE 6, 1950—It is so strange that my strength continues while doing this heavy work and the joy has come back. Arthritis really made gardening hard labor to be done when

I began this year, but the old joy has come back which I thought never would again.

DECEMBER 5—Really I find the young more enjoyable than most people of my age. Some do get so blamed doleful. What if one is drawing near to the end of this life? The change will doubtless be as interesting as any great thing that comes— or if we sleep that is good too. Naturally deafness and arthritis make me resigned—but how I dislike long faces! You will enjoy this:

> Of three
> Who sat in the dooryard sun,
> One said, "I'd like a hill
> When this is done,
> A place where I can look around,
> Provided I'm not sleeping sound."
>
> And one,
> "Hill or vale, what's that to me?
> I'd like a place beneath a tree
> And when the spring is here about,
> I'd climb up with the sap and shout."
>
> But the third said,
> "I'll take a dip in the old woodlot
> Where I can lie in peace and rot,
> Until, someday, as these things go,
> Someone will pinch my dust, just so,
> And say, 'Why man, this stuff will grow.' "
> —Albert Frederick Wilson

JANUARY 10, 1951—I've been enjoying staying alone, doing the many necessary things in an unhurried way. With the New Year a new spirit has come to me—strange with all the sorrow, worldwide and personal, yet something, almost a radiant strength has come, when so needed. If we could but give that sort of thing to another. . . . Dear my child, this reads a stupid letter, and reading is a letter's proof. But I've been doing the hordes of things any old lady does, who knows there are no relatives to step in if she steps out. Then it helps in the spring!

FEBRUARY 1--Who wrote this lovely verse?

> To see a world in a grain of sand,
> And a heaven in a wild flower;
> Hold infinity in the palm of your hand,
> And eternity in an hour.

The little Boston terrier is a source of joy. He gazes at me with bug eyes full of love, quiet as can be till the bell rings when he literally barks his hind feet off the floor. Me, I'm somewhat noisy and I love the din and friskiness.

Now dear blessed, I'll say good-bye. Please never place me among the saints, nor quite among the lost sheep; find a common denominator, do, so I'll be comfortable. Meantime, I welcome light and more than appreciate your expressions of daughterness. «

» FEBRUARY 9, 1951—You may already have heard of Alice Adams Currier's death, but we wanted to make sure. She was staying with her cousin and was, as far as anyone knew, in perfect health. Her son had been there during the evening and she went to bed as usual, feeling fine. The next morning she didn't come down at breakfast time and after a while Grace went up to see if she was all right. She was lying just as she went to sleep and had passed on sometime during the night. For someone living alone as she did she will be missed by more people than anyone I know. A wonderful woman!

Most sincerely,
Alice Adams «

NO MOURNING, PLEASE

Occasionally a newspaper carries a story of a death that surely no one could wish changed, not even the husband's attitude. At least my reaction was: what a happy relationship, what a fitting end!

» LONDON, (AP)—Prof. L. Dudley Stamp was asked recently about one of the most unconventional death announcements ever to appear in the obituary columns of *The London Times*. The notice, which Professor Stamp had inserted after the death of his wife, said:

"Stamp—At sunset on the cliffs of Widemouth in the driving seat of her Humber Snipe, a cigarette half-smoked, *The Times* crossword puzzle nearly completed, Elsa, for 39 years beloved wife and companion of Prof. L. Dudley Stamp. No mourning, please."

Professor Stamp is an economist, geographer, and authority on soil erosion. About the notice he put in the newspaper he said, "It may sound like a penny novelette, but I had a girl pupil once, and the only way I succeeded in teaching her anything was by marrying her. We had a wonderful life together. Five years ago she had a heart attack, but with the aid of drugs she made a good recovery. But we both knew the end might come anytime."

He added that his wife, a religious woman, often prayed that she would die before her husband, and that it would be quick. "That's just the way it happened," Professor Stamp continued. "She recently achieved two of her great ambitions. Our son Brian was married and she made a trip to New Zealand. She was supremely happy."

On the day of her death, he and his wife had driven to a favorite spot to watch the sunset. "It was a beautiful sunset," he said. "We watched it together and were just doing the crossword together. She was smoking at the time. Suddenly the cigarette dropped. I picked it up. She was gone."

Asked why he chose the unusual way of announcing her death, Professor Stamp replied, "Why not, I wanted all her friends to know just how easily, quickly, and simply she went. I think she would have approved." «

THEY WHO WAIT FOR THE LORD

Gertrude Allen's dedication to the mission field was an early influence in the life of a friend of mine who later also became a missionary. Because of Mrs. Allen's heroic acceptance of increasing infirmity and approaching death, she affected all who knew her personally and her example will continue to inspire people in everwidening areas. Her death was reported in *The Houston Post* on June 25, 1964 in an article appearing under the heading "Mrs. Allen Loses 26-Year MS Battle."

"Multiple sclerosis first attacked Mrs. Gertrude Allen in 1938, while she was in China teaching music at Central China University, as a missionary for the Evangelical and Reformed Church. She carried on her work despite the slowly spreading ravages of this little-known disease. For the last 10 years she had been in a wheelchair."

In China, Gertrude Zenk had married Walter Allen, a missionary and the son of missionaries. After communist pressures forced the Allens and their adopted son to return to the United States in 1951, they lived in Wisconsin, Florida, and for two years in Houston, Texas, where Dr. Allen is associated with the University of Houston as adviser to its many international students. Wherever Gertrude went she was an active member of church and civic groups, and for a time directed a junior choir from her wheelchair.

Two days after her death, Dr. Allen wrote a letter that was mimeographed and sent to his wife's friends:

» He gives power to the faint,
and to him who has no might he increases strength.

. . . .

They who wait for the Lord shall renew their strength,
they shall mount up with wings like eagles,
   they shall run and not be weary;
they shall walk and not faint.
                                                —Isaiah 40:29, 31

Gertrude is no longer waiting for the Lord, but while she was waiting she was given power and increased strength of spirit to mount above the confinement of her illness and her wheelchair. On June 24 she was released from the struggle, the pain, the frustration of living with MS for twenty-six years. But she is remembered by her many friends whose lives she touched in Wisconsin, in China, in New York, in Miami, and recently in Houston. Those who learned of her illness during the past three weeks have sent in a flood of testimony to the splendid example of courage, cheer, and faith that her life has been. Friends from the church, the neighborhood, the university, gave many hours of care as a sign of the love they had for her.

Although Gertrude made a marvelous recovery from her cancer operation last September, she never fully regained her previous abilities. . . . Her doctor put her in St. Luke's Hospital on May 31. . . . On June 12 he said we could bring her home, as we could do as much for her here as was possible at the hospital. Our devoted housekeeper, Mrs. Thomas, took over twenty-four-hour nursing duties. . . . On June 23 Gertrude fell asleep at noon and she did not wake again.

Gertrude had always wanted to have her body donated to the scientific study of multiple sclerosis so that she might be of help to future sufferers of the disease. Arrangements were made for her body to be given to the Baylor University

College of Medicine. A memorial service was held at 10:30 A.M. on June 25 at Westbury Methodist Church, where she had worshiped almost every Sunday for the past two years. . . . A memorial to Gertrude will be the altar in the new sanctuary of this church. . . .

Mother Allen flew in from California as soon as she heard of Gertrude's illness, and she is staying on . . . to help through this period of destitution and loneliness. With the memory of Gertrude to sustain us, with her example before us, and with her friends to support us, we shall try to continue her spirit of cheerful service. We must not sorrow, because Gertrude has graduated through death to an immortal life of peace. «

From a recent book and from an old, old pre-Christian one come two examples of men condemned to die—one by war; one by jury.

Thanks to Ernest Gordon we know how Scots soldiers held as prisoners of war by the Japanese moved from death-camp despair to spiritual triumph, and how one young Argyle in particular died without fear.

Thanks to Plato the wisdom of Socrates was preserved for future generations.

FRIENDS HELP

» I was walking back to my hut one evening when a medical orderly from the hospital stopped me. "Excuse me, sir," he said. "There's an Argyle in my ward who'd like to see you. . . . He's a young lad." . . .

"Does he need massage?"

"No. There's nothing we can do. He's dying. He has gangrene. It's all through him."

"What would you like me to do, then?"

"He's so miserable, I thought perhaps you could comfort

him. In any case, he'll be glad to see another Argyle." . . .

The orderly must have been accustomed to seeing youngsters die. But something about this one seemed to have touched him. The dim light accentuated both the boy's youth and his loneliness.

"Here he is, lad," the orderly said softly. "I've brought him to you."

Large, frightened gray eyes stared up at me from an emaciated face. I bent closer. He seemed to recognize me.

"Oh, I'm so glad to see you, sir. . . . I've been so lonely. I don't know anyone here. It's been a long time since I've seen an Argyle. . . . I've become terribly depressed. I suppose because I'm . . . so scared at times I can't think." . . .

What could I say? I knew he didn't have a chance because of the advanced state of his gangrene. I looked at him, lying there so lonely and so young, and said the only thing I could think of, "We'll help you not to be scared. We'll stay by you."

That seemed to ease his mind. . . . I did what I could for him, but it hurt because it was so little. I passed the word to Dusty and Dinty. They went to see him often, and in turn, encouraged their friends to do so. Soon the lad had a chain of regular visitors; he did not spend too many hours alone.

I had been able to obtain some delicacies for him—a duck egg and half a hand of bananas. I went to take these to him. . . . I was delighted at the change in his manner. He seemed relaxed and almost cheerful. . . .

"You've no idea what a help it is to have friends. I don't feel lonely anymore. And I'm not scared. . . . I'm going to die, am I not?"

I cleared my throat, searching for words. "That's a possibility we all have to face. I've faced it—so have a lot of others."

"I know." The boy nodded. "That's why I like to talk to you. You've been through it. You understand."

I did not answer. I was thinking to myself, "Do I? Do I? Can I ever understand even a little of what goes on in another's mind and heart?" . . .

"It's hard to be young and to have to die. I don't even know what this war is all about."

"Here, let me read you something that may help." I spoke the words evenly, pretending to be more in control of my emotions than I actually was. I had brought my Bible with me. I opened its torn pages and in the dim light of the hut I began to read those words that had brought solace to countless souls before him:

"Yea, though I walk through the valley of the shadow of death, I will fear no evil: for thou art with me; thy rod and thy staff they comfort me."

I looked at him. He was lying quietly. I turned to another passage: "I am the resurrection, and the life: he that believeth in me, though he were dead, yet shall he live: and whosoever liveth and believeth in me shall never die. Believest thou this?"

I put the Bible down. His gray eyes were far away. . . . After a bit he turned his gaze into mine and said with prefect calm, "Everything is going to be all right."

"Yes," I said, nodding, "everything is going to be all right."

He slumped back. His efforts had exhausted him. I knelt beside his sleeping platform and gently stroked his forehead with my fingers until he fell into a deep, untroubled sleep.

Two evenings later . . . I saw the orderly coming toward me on the run.

"Quickly!" he cried. "He hasn't long to go." . . .

I knelt beside him and took his pathetically thin hand in mine. A yellow glow lighted up the darkness behind me. The thoughtful orderly had produced a coconut-oil lamp.

"Light," said the boy in his low voice. "It's good to have light. I don't like the dark." . . . "It's all right. I'm glad it's all right," he whispered. There was a look of trust and hope on his face as he said this.

"Yes, my son, it's all right," I assured him. "God our Father is with us. He is very near." . . . Still holding his hand, I prayed, "Our Father which art in heaven, hallowed be thy name. . . ."

His eyes were closed. But as I watched his face I could see his lips repeating the words with me.

"Thy kingdom come. . . ."

The lamp grew dim, then burned more brightly.

"Thy will be done in earth, as it is in heaven. . . ."

His lips no longer moved. His breath started coming in great sobbing gasps. They ceased. He was quiet—with the quietness of death.

"Father," I prayed, "receive this dear child. Welcome him with thy love for the sake of Jesus Christ, our Savior, thy Son. Amen." . . .

It was experiences such as these that made our discussions in the bamboo grove meaningful. . . . We were learning what it means to be alive—to be human. As we became more aware of our responsibility to God the Father, we realized that we were put in this world not to be served but to serve. This truth touched and influenced many of us to some degree, even those who shunned any religious quest. There was a general reawakening. Men began to smile—even to laugh and to sing . . . "Jerusalem the Golden." . . . The song made the darkness seem friendly. In the difference between this joyful sound and the joyless stillness of months past was the difference between life and death.

This hymn had the sound of victory. To me it said: "Man need never be so defeated that he can do nothing. Weak, sick, broken in body, far from home, and alone in a strange land, he can sing! He can worship!"

The resurgence of life increased. It grew and leavened the whole camp, expressing itself in men's concern for their neighbors. «

THE WISDOM OF SOCRATES

» You too, gentlemen of the jury, must look forward to death with confidence, and fix your minds on this one belief, which is certain: that nothing can harm a good man either in life or after death, and his fortunes are not a matter of indifference to the gods. This present experience of mine has not come about mechanically; I am quite clear that the time had come when it was better for me to die and be released from my distractions. That is why my sign never turned me back. For my own part I bear no grudge at all against those who condemned me and accused me, although it was not with this kind intention that they did so, but because they thought that they were hurting me; and that is culpable of them. However, I ask them to grant me one favor. When my sons grow up, gentlemen, if you think that they are putting money or anything else before goodness, take your revenge by plaguing them as I plagued you; and if they fancy themselves for no reason, you must scold them just as I scolded you, for neglecting the important things and thinking that they are good for something when they are good for nothing. If you do this, I shall have had justice at your hands, both I myself and my children.

Now it is time that we were going, I to die and you to live; but which of us has the happier prospect is unknown to anyone but God. «

CHAPTER FIVE

A Time to Speak

FOR EVERYTHING there is a season, and a time for every matter under heaven:
  a time to be born, and a time to die;
  a time to plant, and a time to pluck up what is planted;
  a time to kill, and a time to heal;
  a time to break down, and a time to build up;
  a time to weep, and a time to laugh;
  a time to mourn, and a time to dance;
  a time to cast away stones, and a time to gather stones
    together;
  a time to embrace, and a time to refrain from embracing;
  a time to seek, and a time to lose;
  a time to keep, and a time to cast away;
  a time to rend, and a time to sew;
  a time to keep silence, and a time to speak.

—Ecclesiastes 3:1-7

Several times a year I go to see old Mrs. G who has outlived all the rest of her family. One of four sisters, she was the only one to marry. And a very happy marriage it was, though there were no children and her husband died in middle age. She returned to her childhood neighborhood

where she became the homemaker for her three maiden
sisters. The frail one had a long illness and was lovingly
cared for by Mrs. G. After her death, the three who were
left had many pleasant years together until a lingering illness took the shopkeeping sister. The nurse sister long had
had an impaired heart and at last became bedfast. She too
was tenderly nursed for months that ran into years. After
her death, Mrs. G was literally the last leaf on the family
tree. For over five years now she has been in a nursing
home, confined to her bed.

While there are no relatives, her friends are faithful; two
of them visit her regularly each week; others make the fif-
teen-mile trip for special occasions. Mrs. G is greatly beloved because she is still a good listener: "Tell me about the
children. Tell me about your trip. Tell me what blooms in
your garden."

Her mind is clear and keen. One day this tiny, ninety-
year-old woman with arthritic hands so twisted she cannot
hold a book or a fork, asked a favor: "Would you please copy
for me Browning's 'Rabbi Ben Ezra'—

> Grow old along with me!
> The best is yet to be,
> The last of life, for which the first was made.
> Our times are in his hand.

—I must not remember it correctly, or else he did not know
what he was talking about. Here I lie, year after year, listening to the whimpers of my roommates. I so long to die. Why
can't my old heart stop beating? Why can't I slip away?"

In comparison to many forsaken old people who have
neither relatives nor friends, who lie in beds less clean in
rooms where there are six or more patients instead of three,
my old friend is fortunate.

Young and middle-aged couples who invite a parent to

live with them, or who try to care for an invalid mother or
father in today's small houses and without help usually end
the experience with a sense of failure rather than a feeling
of being blessed by a parent's company. There is no one
right, easy solution. Grown-up children who realize the limitations of their house, their strength, their patience, and
therefore place their parents in an institution often suffer
remorse.

The Bushman in the Kalahari Desert forced to leave behind the weak old ones of his family because of insufficient
food, left them with grief and out of necessity. If game was
discovered, runners were sent back to bring in the stragglers.
Their feast became a reunion of rejoicing.

Christian peoples have long sat in judgment on primitive
tribes who abandon their weak and helpless old people. How
heartless, we say, to walk away and desert a toothless Eskimo
crone in a snowdrift. Look at us, we would not forsake a
human being no matter how useless. We will keep alive each
of God's children as long as possible.

Is this concern based on a premise that the body is more
precious than the spirit, that life as we know it is a value
that must be preserved as long as medically possible? Have
we modern Christians vaunted the worth of the body and
thereby rejected belief in a life after death, belief that death
is but a turn in the road on the long journey of the soul's
pilgrimage from self to God?

Present-day culture in these United States psychically
casts off its old people as completely as pagan primitives
deserted their ancients. Countless agencies and institutions
are set up to serve our elders. But a social worker with the
department of public assistance does well to visit each "case"
twice a year. "Senior citizens" who are curious, adventure-
some, friendly, and in good health discover new satisfactions

in their days of retirement. But many not so fortunate withdraw into themselves, fear new experiences, or are physically handicapped. Such poor creatures, stubborn in spirit, or broken in body, are forgotten by society but linger on because of adequate food and drugs. They are rejected emotionally as completely as ever the primitive ancient was rejected physically.

Humanity scorns and condemns the Nazis who performed experimental operations on the Polish women, known as the Lapins. But our doctors, who intravenously feed old shells and transfuse blood into old veins, are respected; they are doing all that scientific knowledge has discovered to keep the heart beating, whether or not there is any mind to enjoy life, or a desire to live. There was a time when pneumonia was known as the old man's friend. Now too few are allowed to die naturally, to slip away peacefully into their eternal home.

Occasionally there is a happy exception. When old Mrs. Martin was in her last illness she implored her daughter, "Do not send me to a hospital; please let me die at home."

No doubt there had been difficult days with three generations under one roof, but they had managed to live together for ten years with affectionate regard; the young couple decided after talking to their physician that they could weather the next several weeks until their mother was set free.

This household was fortunate to have had a family doctor who could speak honestly: "If I send your mother to the hospital she will have excellent care; she will be fed whether or not she is hungry; every effort will be made to keep her heart beating. If you keep her here you will have constant washing and continuous running up and down stairs. It will be hard for you, but your mother can die naturally."

THE MINISTER SPEAKS

On March 17, 1963 in the Central Methodist Church of Lansing, Michigan, our friend Dwight S. Large preached on the theme "These Are the Blessed: the Merciful." The sermon was transcribed; the introduction follows.

» One aspect of our religion you and I resist; you and I dislike facing the truth about ourselves. It's much easier to hold a mirror up for someone else to look and see his situation, what he ought to do about it, than to look into the mirror directly. . . . Worship at its best should have self-examination, and I am asking you to examine this difficulty in order that we might grapple with one aspect of the truth that we ordinarily deny. It is this: that with all the outward evidences which might cause one to believe that we are closely tied together, in our modern society, actually and tragically we are separated, one from another. We are cut off in a very meaningful and tragic way from one another!

We live closer together in cities and suburbs than our fathers. We work closer in factories and offices, but the physical proximity does not cover up the truth which is that we are individually separated. We're cut off. We find it difficult to communicate with one another about things that matter. We don't talk about these deep hungers of the spirit— those questions such as who we are and why we are here, and where we are going. We don't talk about our fears.

The last five funerals I have conducted were all preceded by a conference with the members of the family of the deceased. As is always our custom, I brought up the question, "Were there any requests, were there any suggestions ever discussed by the family for this kind of break in the family circle?" With one exception, all the others said: This is something we never talked about in our family; we never heard Dad, or Mother, or brother—whatever the case was—ever express himself in terms of what he was thinking about dying. No, we live years closely tied together in a family unit but not communicating with one another on things that matter.

I remember Steve once woke my awareness when he said one day, "Dad, do you ever realize how many people spend so much time as they do talking about the weather?" So I watched for a week. We talk "How do you do—I'm fine, how are you?" patter. I remember an elderly senior citizen in Philadelphia who disliked the casual conversation based on "How are you today?" When anyone asked this question she spoke clearly with a blunt reply, "If you really want to know, I don't feel well today, and I don't mind telling you the truth!" We talk outwardly, but we don't put ourselves into it—our true selves. The beatniks have an expressive phrase which gathers my meaning in deep focus; the beatniks say, "Are you with it?"—meaning your real self.

In the speaking, in the listening, we talk, but we're cut off from one another—we find it difficult to discuss things that really matter. «

Many years ago a book of great wisdom, *The Negro Spiritual Speaks of Life and Death,* was my introduction to Howard Thurman. In *Deep River* he continues to stress the imponderables shaping our existence—life and death and love.

» From the hospital, the deceased is carried to a place of preparation for burial, the mortuary. . . . The result is that death has been largely alienated from the normal compass of daily experience. Our sense of personal loss may be great but our primary relationship with death under normal circumstances tends to be impersonal and detached. We shrink from direct personal contact with death. It is very difficult for us to handle the emotional upsets growing out of our experience with death when we are denied the natural moments of exhaustive reaction which are derivatives of the performance of last personal services for the dead. Therapeutic effects are missed. Tremendous emotional blocks are set up without release, making for devious forms of inner chaos, which cause us to limp through the years with our griefs unassuaged.

This was not the situation with the creators of the spirituals. Their contact with the dead was immediate, inescapable, dramatic. The family or friends washed the body of the dead, the grave clothes were carefully and personally selected or especially made. The coffin itself was built by a familiar hand. It may have been a loving though crude device, or an expression of genuine, first-class craftsmanship. During all these processes, the body remained in the home— first wrapped in cooling sheets and then "laid out" for the time interval before burial. . . .

But the great idea about death itself is that it is not *the master of life.* It may be inevitable, yes; gruesome, perhaps; releasing, yes; but triumphant, *never.* With such an affirmation ringing in their ears, it became possible for them, slaves though they were, to stand anything that life could bring against them. «

> » Wade in the water,
> Wade in the water, children,
> God is going to trouble the waters.

What is the meaning of this? What are they trying to say in these simple, insight-laden words? . . . They are suggesting that in all the troubles of life, in all the experiences of life, there is an inner and binding logic that causes the particular experience in and of itself to be consistent; therefore rational. [These early singers] took the imagery of the simple New Testament story and applied it to their own situation.

For them the "troubled waters" meant the ups and downs, the vicissitudes of life. Within the context of the "troubled" waters of life there are healing waters, because God is in the midst of the turmoil. . . .

When we deal with the tragedies of life it is profitable ever to seek to commune, to grapple with all the rational clues that are available. . . . It is quite possible that a person may work at his life problem over what for him is a total time interval, getting more and more insight as the years unfold, with all the richness and mellowness that such an experience would precipitate; at last it begins to dawn deep within the spirit that God, the creative mind and spirit in the core of the universe, is at work.

This leads to a very searching insight. Here we are face to face with perhaps the most daring and revolutionary concept known to man: namely, that God is not only the creative mind and spirit at the core of the universe but that he—and mark you, I say he—is love. There are no completely satisfying ways by which this conclusion may be arrived at by mere or sheer rational reflective processes. This is the great disclosure: that there is at the heart of life a Heart. When such an insight is possessed by the human spirit and possesses the human spirit, a vast and awe-inspiring tranquillity irradiates the life. This is the message of the spiritual. Do not shrink from moving confidently out into the choppy seas. Wade in the water, because God is troubling the water. «

THE DOCTOR SPEAKS

Paul Tournier is a French medical doctor, a psychiatrist, and a serious student of the Bible. Because he combines scientific knowledge with religious faith his books are widely read in the United States as well as in Europe.

In *A Doctor's Casebook in the Light of the Bible,* Dr.

Tournier describes an investigation among two hundred patients who were asked what they expected from a doctor. First and foremost they hoped to be cured, but more than this "they wanted the doctor to pay real attention to their suffering and distress, to treat them as human beings and not as guinea pigs, and to tell them the truth about their disease, about its probable duration, and what his prognosis was. The desire to be told the truth was put first." But many of them qualified this by asking not to be cowed and shocked, but to be told gently and tactfully so that they might be helped to accept the truth. Dr. Tournier adds:

» I must . . . confess that I have not always been able to tell a patient seriously ill what I thought about his condition. And I have always had in such cases . . . a feeling of failure and guilt. But I . . . have always felt that my fault lay further back, . . . when the patient was not so near death, to establish close contact with him and to create that climate of spiritual fellowship without which the truth cannot be told. It is in speaking of the meaning of things that we enter into this fellowship, giving the patient an opportunity of talking to us about the things that are weighing on his mind, long before he reaches the last extremity. Since every sickness is a reminder of our mortal state, it is easy to recall this biblical meaning of disease before it has become serious. We speak then of death as the great unknown, for which we must all be ready, doctor as well as patient; for, after all, who can be certain that I shall not die before my patient does?

But let us admit it: there is a streak of cowardice in all of us, doctors and patients alike; each one of us . . . puts up a stubborn resistance against tackling the essential, tragic, and insoluble problems of suffering, disease, and death. This honest man-to-man discussion . . . requires courage to start and to continue without hedging. It inevitably brings up problems in which the doctor himself is often in the dark. There are many doctors who hold high professional ideals, who long with all their hearts to profess a humane medicine. But can they, without a religious faith? For if they are not fully convinced that their own life has a meaning, how can they approach the questions their patients put to them about human destiny? It is then that they are so easily tempted to change the subject of conversation. . . .

So, when the disease is not serious, it is easy to avoid the problem of death, and to keep up the morale by assuring the patient of his recovery. . . . As long as this is probable, all is well. But when it becomes improbable, . . . it is too late then to call on quite different moral resources, grounded in faith, which give the patient courage to look reality in the face. . . .

A brother doctor whom a surgical operation has snatched from otherwise certain death [writes]: "To you I can say . . . I really feel that Providence intervened, wishing to make me understand that I am being allowed to go on living for a very special purpose. That will lay many obligations upon me, and so I shall be very much in need of the continued prayers of friends like you."

So, if we are the kind of doctors we ought to be, not absorbed entirely by the technical problems of the case, but having a care for the patient as a person, if we penetrate with affection into the secret places of his heart, where he is troubled by the problems of the meaning of sickness and death, a quiet understanding is established, which deepens as the disease worsens. We feel then that we have not departed from the truth; the patient becomes increasingly aware of the increasing danger without our ever having to break it to him brutally. . . .

This sense of our common destiny establishes a real fellowship between us. These questions about the meaning of illness and death concern us as much as they concern our patient; we are taking part together both in the tragedy of our human condition and in the miracle of salvation.

There is nothing more impressive for the doctor than thus to accompany a patient who has become a dear friend and who is walking in full knowledge of his condition to meet death; a patient who remains human, who does not repress or hide his moments of rebellion or distress, but who at the same time is deepening his blessing of faith. «

I have been heartened that in the last several years frank presentations on the subject of dying have appeared in popular magazines and daily newspapers. Three such accounts follow:

» When a patient is dying—whether from inoperable cancer in the prime of life, or from a degenerative disease of old age—Dr. Walter C. Alvarez prescribes kindness in two forms: frankness and indulgence.

Dr. Alvarez, 66, famed Mayo Clinic diagnostician, is editor of *GP*, monthly journal of the American Academy of General Practice. Addressing general practitioners . . . Alvarez counseled against lying to a dying patient or keeping up a cheerful farce for his supposed benefit. In one way or another, the patient usually finds out or guesses what his condition is, and then his miseries are increased by annoyance at the dissembling physician. Sometimes the victim is not so much appalled by impending death as he is by the prospect of leaving his wife or husband. In that case Alvarez talks frankly to both: "You two know perfectly well what this disease is, so why should you now be lying to one another, as you never did before? Why not now face this hardest of all things together?"

If there is pain, Alvarez believes in giving drugs to the dying patient with the utmost generosity. What if he does become addicted? It will make no difference in his grave. Moreover, naked suffering brings on death more quickly than morphine and other analgesics do.

Alvarez does not prescribe diets for old people except in cases of absolute necessity (e.g., diabetes, severe gout, swelling of the legs). In general he believes in letting oldsters— whether healthy or ill—eat, smoke, and drink what they like. He told of two middle-aged women who brought their spry, neat, 80-year-old father in to see him. Another doctor had found a little high blood pressure, and had deprived the old boy of his pipe, his bedtime highball, his red meat, his table salt, his puttering in the garden and his strolls around town. The father had rebelled and the women wanted Alvarez to back up the other doctor.

Alvarez refused. He assured the women their father would very likely die all the sooner if deprived of his comforts, and have a worse time over it.

"When I myself lie dying," said Dr. Alvarez, "I hope I will have by me some wise, kindly physician who will keep interns from frequently pulling me up to examine my chest, or from constantly puncturing my veins, or from giving me enemas or drastic medicines. I am sure that at the end I will very much want to be left alone." «

» Does it mean death when a man's heart stops, or is there reasonable hope that the vital organ can be started up again to bring back life? When a doctor is confronted with this dread question, he must make up his mind instantly. He usually has only five minutes at most to restore circulation before the brain cells die.

If the doctor assesses the emergency correctly and acts soon enough, he can use remarkable new resuscitation techniques to bring back a complete human personality from what previous generations considered to be death. But some doctors, overestimating the power of science, are opposing the dark angel when there is no real hope for success. They hold off death, but cannot restore life. Their patients live as a carrot lives, with no thought, no feeling, and no expectation of ever thinking or feeling. They linger on in hospital beds, unable truly to live again and prevented by science from dying.

When it is pointed out to these doctors what a nightmare this is for grieving families, they invariably say that the oath of the great physician of ancient Greece, Hippocrates, to which physicians and surgeons adhere, requires them to preserve life at all costs. They insist that it is their duty to use extraordinary methods even when death is irreversible. I am convinced that their ill-fated efforts result from a serious misinterpretation of the Hippocratic oath, ignorance of what religion teaches, an excess of pride in modern techniques, even confusion as to what life and death are. . . .

There is no doubt that every physician is obligated to fight for his patient's life while there is any hope that he can defeat death. When he takes the Hippocratic oath, he swears, "I will follow that method of treatment which, according to my ability and judgment, I consider for the benefit of my patients and abstain from whatever is deleterious and wrong." How can it be judged to be to the benefit of a patient to cheat him of peace while being powerless to restore him to consciousness? Only a person who thinks of human life in terms of a senseless specimen of protoplasm in a test tube can see any merit in such a course. After all, consciousness alone means life to human beings.

Hippocrates lived about 2,500 years ago, and he scarcely could have imagined the ingenious machines of today which can take up the vital work of the heart and lungs. He could not have foreseen the ethical problems posed by their use. When these machines are used wisely, doctors save lives. They can restore what a few years ago would have been a dead man to the full enjoyment of life. But they cannot be used with impunity to reverse the ebb of life when it has passed beyond the point of irreversibility.

Sometimes in the operating room, drugs, anesthesia, or the shock of surgery will cause a heart to stop beating. Then the doctor is required by sound medical practice to use every device and technique to bring back his patient's pulse and breathing if he can. But he must do so within inexorable time limits set by nature. . . .

When an accident stops the heart, there is good reason to believe the patient can be restored without damage to the brain. Doctors and laymen alike are bound to act on this assumption. But if death results from a disease, there is little hope of reversing it. At a New York hospital a man died of pneumonia, but the doctors would not admit defeat. Even though the patient's tissues were perishing, they started up the weary heart and lungs again and succeeded in keeping them going mechanically for several days before a second death took place. In the face of irreversible death such conduct is at best an illogical and ritualistic gesture.

It would have been better to have allowed the patient to pass away, as we recently did a terminal cancer case at Cook County Hospital. He was a man in his fifties, suffering from cancer of the pharynx. In the last year it had spread to his neck and jaw and was now obstructing his windpipe. Finally he could no longer breathe. A tube was inserted to provide oxygen to keep him alive. But we knew there was no hope. When it became apparent that he had passed beyond the point of return, the situation was explained to his family. He was near death, could never recover, and only the machine kept him alive. The relatives tearfully asked that the extraordinary methods be discontinued. The machine was removed, and the man died. . . .

An unconscious person who can never regain consciousness and who can only remain tenuously alive with the assistance of machines is to all human purposes dead. He is still alive biologically, of course, because biological death occurs only as the cells of the body die. Death occurs at different times in different cells and organs. Both the pneumonia and cancer patients passed the point of clinical death, only to have their biological death postponed by the action of machines. When it became evident that the patients could not recover and that, in fact, their systems were continuing to decline, one group of doctors chose to play God. We chose instead to accept the decision of God. «

» The Most Rev. Fulton J. Sheen said Sunday he found no moral need for "extraordinary means" to prolong the life of a dying patient, but that such means should be considered if the patient's family desires it. In such cases, however, said the Auxiliary Bishop of the Archdiocese of New York, "I would counsel the family to take the advice of the doctor."

Bishop Sheen's remarks came at a press conference held jointly with Dr. Edward R. Rynearson of the Mayo Clinic in Rochester, Minnesota, at the opening of the 112th annual meeting of the American Medical Association.

At last year's AMA meeting, Dr. Rynearson startled the medical profession by assailing the use of unusual means to extend the lives of hopeless cancer patients. He reiterated the position Sunday. Such extraordinary means would include the use of numerous tubes, oxygen equipment, or other apparatus to keep alive a patient for whom there is no hope of improvement. Dr. Rynearson cited as an example the widow of a prominent millionaire who was kept alive for

11 years in a totally unconscious state. "If anyone can take pride in that, let them," he said.

Asked whether unusual means of prolonging life are "morally necessary," Bishop Sheen said, "No, particularly if the family did not ask for it. If I were dying, with my body full of tubes and there was no way to move, I would ask [the doctor] to take them out," the bishop continued. "I see no moral issue here."

Both men emphasized that they were not speaking of so-called mercy killing in which a patient's life is deliberately ended. They agreed on a moral requirement to use all "ordinary" means to sustain life.

Appearing on an evening program on the role of medicine and religion in the "total care" of the patient, the two men agreed that physical and spiritual ailments are related and that both aspects must be considered. Dr. Rynearson also said he believed that "strong religious beliefs protect people from tension and anxieties which might damage or destroy them if they had no such beliefs," and that a physician will "be better able to help his patients" if the doctor has a strong religious faith. «

THE COMMUNITY SPEAKS

In days gone by a neighbor or relative of the family washed and laid out the person who had fallen on his last sleep. The farewell service was then held in the home or in the church where young and old had worshiped together, were christened and married, where strength for the coming week had been found each Sunday.

Nowadays most undertakers will find one reason after another to explain why it is not feasible to hold a funeral in the church or meetinghouse. Modern man has lost a precious heritage in allowing the mortician to capitalize on his personal sorrow and bewilderment, to sell him an expensive casket, to talk him into using a funeral home. If the family will remember to call their minister first, before the undertaker is notified, they will be upheld in their stand to hold the funeral in their accustomed place of worship.

Many people in this country are under the impression that embalming is required by law. It is true that if the body is not embalmed, cremation or burial must take place within twenty-four hours after death. If the custom of viewings could be abandoned, if there were no longer open caskets at the farewell service, remembrance of the beloved dead would be remembrance of them as they were alive. Who of us, even though we went through this painful ordeal of looking at our parents laid out in their coffins, now picture them in our minds as we saw them there? Or if there is any measure of comfort to be had by seeing again our loved ones in the peace and repose of death, is this not better accomplished in the privacy of the family rather than before onlookers?

That which we have in our hearts can never be taken from us. My memory is stored with scenes in which my parents move and breathe, laugh and talk. I see my father calling in the sheep, promising us that we might claim the little black lambs. I see my mother mending at the upstairs window of our house, watching and waving us a welcome as we straggle in from school. The depth and dignity of a memorial service so often brings such memories to our minds with a new awareness of their worth.

Instead of allowing ourselves to be influenced by the mortician or swayed by public opinion, would we not better show our love and respect for our dear ones if relatives and friends gathered together for a memorial service in the church some days after the body was cremated or buried?

Would it not be more of a religious service, a meeting for worship, where those who mourn would be given strength to walk the lonesome road that stretches endlessly ahead, where the dead would be remembered with love and thanksgiving?

Should we not give thought to the disposition of our own bodies? Some people will their eyes to eye banks so that corneal transplants can restore sight to the blind. Some individuals will their bodies to the local anatomical board for medical experimentation. By furthering research one's usefulness can continue after death.

In some communities, groups of concerned people have formed themselves into funeral or memorial societies. These societies often share their ideas through the Continental Association of Funeral and Memorial Societies located in Chicago, Illinois. The suggestions and purposes of the various groups are similar. The Indianapolis, Indiana organization has established these general principles:

» 1. We suggest the consideration of cremation. Cremation brings about the inevitable dissolution of the remains cleanly, quickly, and at low cost.

Long custom, and in some cases religious injunction, may support ground burial. Where burial is preferred, the ceremony should be private, dignified, and of the utmost simplicity. Embalming is not necessary for such immediate disposition, either by cremation or by burial. The purchase of expensive caskets, monuments, urns, or burial plots is not a measure of regard or affection for the dead. Where simple dignity and the simplest arrangements are maintained, attention may be wholly directed to the spiritual values implicit in the experience of death.

2. We suggest that the showing of the corpse be avoided. The custom of "viewing the remains" is not only unnecessary

but in most cases anguishing, and in all cases needlessly expensive.

3. We suggest that any service prior to cremation or burial should be private, to be followed, when desired, by a memorial service. The traditional funeral service comes when grief is fresh and physical separation uppermost in the mind. A memorial service can be arranged with enough leisure to allow the family to regain a measure of composure.

If a funeral service is held it should emphasize thanksgiving for the essential goodness of the dead. The service is best held in the church or family place of worship.

[The saving of money is only one facet in the arrangements at the time of death; the aim is to preserve dignity and simplicity in all things connected with rites for the dead.]

4. We suggest that sympathy be expressed by some gift to a fund or cause in which the deceased had an active interest. Most institutions are prepared to send an acknowledgment to the family stating that a gift has been received. The family of the bereaved should state in the funeral notice the specific charities and causes which were dear to the deceased.

[If flowers are sent, it is preferable to send them to the home where their beauty and fragrance comfort the living rather than to the grave to decorate the dead. Cut flowers, or potted plants, rather than floral arrangements, can be better shared with others.] «

THE NOVELIST SPEAKS

I am a reader of novels, discovering spiritual insights in those that are worth rereading. *The River Garden of Pure Repose* by Grace Boynton is now out of print, but it continues to speak to me. The book begins and ends with a

quotation from the fourteenth-century mystic Meister Eck-
hart. Some of the principal characters are Jane Breasted,
who is dying; Wilfreda Grayson, her nurse; Jack Fernald, an
army pilot; and Stephen Purcell, a conscientious objector to
war.

» *Wilfreda Grayson:* Of course she gives these people no
hint of her real situation and talks as if she had a normal life-
span before her. I marvel that she can care about such things
as the affairs of other folk, and Chinese garden architecture,
forsooth! After she had read me her reply to Dr. Manners'
letter, she looked at me and laughed.

"You are puzzled," she accused me. "You are saying to
yourself, Jane is on the brink of eternity—so for heaven's
sake, why Chinese rock work—now aren't you?"

"Yes," I admitted it.

"My dear," Jane reached her hand to me. "Do you know
why you are a comfort to me? In many ways, of course; but
the great thing is that I may speak freely with you about the
end of Brother Ass. He is on the brink of death and subse-
quent corruption; but you know as I do that myself am in
for no such things. I stand on no brink at all. I am at home
—here or hereafter."

Tears were in the eyes of us both. But Jane having asserted
that I comprehend her, I do so increasingly, if blunderingly.
I have heard that the true mystic is usually silent about his
inner life. This seems to apply to her. I am glad she . . . can
speak freely to me, but even so, she has very little to say
about herself. . . .

Jane, a soul poised for flight . . . turns to me because I see
death as she does—not as a pit of darkness but as an opening into Light. This makes it possible for my dear one to
show her inmost self to me.

.   .   .

Jack Fernald was going nuts. That was the way he put it to himself. . . . He did not notice where he went, nor how long he walked. . . . He found himself standing under a roof carried on pillars. . . . There was a house, or a sort of room, mostly paper-backed lattice. . . . He didn't notice more because a voice then said, "Hello there." . . .

Fernald stared and stammered, "Hello," but he couldn't say anything more for a moment. He could only look. And the face in the chair looked at him. At last he remembered something about manners and brought out: "I'm sorry. . . . I didn't know anyone was here."

"No," said the voice. "Of course not. I haven't been here very long myself." Then the eyes shut, the face went dreadfully white, and he saw that it was in pain.

"Can I do anything? Shall I go away?" . . .

"Don't go. Sit down." Soon the face in the chair spoke again, "The pain is gone now." . . .

"It was mighty bad, wasn't it?"

"Yes. It comes, but it goes again. I wouldn't have spoken about it, but you saw. Perhaps you and I are in the same boat?" . . .

"How did you know?"

"How did you know when my pain came on me? When it is bad, pain shows. I have one kind. You have another."

His face began to twitch.

"We can't talk about this to people who are not in our place," the voice went on. "But I see by your uniform that you are a pilot; you see that I am ill and can't recover. We both face death, and we can speak of it to each other. I don't think you'll 'go nuts' anymore."

"You don't? A fat lot . . ." He stopped.

"Yes. To other people you could say 'a fat lot you know about it.' But you can't say that to me. I do know." . . .

"Say, you told me you can't get well. Are you sure?"

"As sure as my doctors and my best friends are. They think it may be about three months now."

"And you think so yourself?"

"I think so myself."

"But you're so quiet . . . so perfectly quiet, that's what you are." He kept repeating it.

She said nothing, and again he felt the lingering quality in her gaze. "It's your quietness that has got into me. . . . Say, what's the matter with you?"

She told him, and he drew a sharp breath. "God! I've heard of that. They say it's awful: it's the worst . . . can't they do anything about it?"

"Oh yes, they can do a great deal. I shall have help. But in three months I expect I shan't need help anymore. And it's all right." . . .

"You haven't got a chance, . . . what have I got to crab about? At least I've got a chance."

"And you have youth, and strength, and courage."

"Courage? You say that after seeing me as scared as a lost kid in the dark? . . . But you aren't scared."

"No," said Jane. "And neither are you, really. I know you won't go nuts again. You said yourself you are clear now. Think. There is a difference, isn't there?"

.   .   .

"Stephen," [Jane] said, "Brother Ass is behaving himself in a seemly manner at present. And whether he behaves or not, all is well with me. That is what I want my friends to . . . remember."

The water stood in the young man's eyes—he could not tell why. He looked across the pool where the round lily pads were green on the gray surface. Jane continued her work, and changed the subject with her next question.

.   .   .

"God lies in wait for us with nothing so much as love. Love is like a fisherman's hook. Without the hook he could never catch a fish, but once the hook is taken, even though the fish twists hither and yon, still the fisherman is sure of him. And so, too, I speak of love: he who is held by it is held by the strongest of bonds, and yet the stress is pleasant. Moreover, he can sweetly bear all that happens to him. When one has found this bond, he looks for no other.

> The hook of love
> Caught me, long since:
> And when strength failed
> And pain beset me
> Then, on that hook I felt
> The tug of God."
> —Meister Eckhart «

Many people liked Jessamyn West's *The Friendly Persuasion,* and many more were enthusiastic about the motion picture based on the story of the nineteenth-century Indiana Quaker family. But few readers seem to remember the last chapter of the book, "Homer and the Lilies," which is my favorite.

» When Jess was eighty years old, somewhat gnarled, but still a very sturdy man, he came to know for a short time an asylum-boy, as he was called, by the name of Homer Denham. . . . Jess first saw the boy on a fine afternoon toward the close of September. . . .

"Howdy," Jess called across to him. "Come on over. I'm tired looking at fish. Like to rest my eyes on something without fins for a change."

Homer paused for a second, then waded seriously across the stream, . . . stood beside the stump, unspeaking, smiling a little, his black eyes trying to make out what kind of man had hailed him, the pulse in his throat jumping. . . .

Homer was constantly surprised and wanted to speak with someone about what had surprised him. He was filled with wonder at a hundred sights: with the colors a colorless icicle took on when the sun touched it, and the way flames leaped in to attack a hickory burl, then leaped away again as if the burl were fighting for its life; he noted how the smoke on a cool evening curled about the house like a tongue, and the way grass could push a stone over. . . .

Homer leaned against the stump. "Do you think a mouse," he said, "if it had to, could run backward?"

Jess pulled his hat down over his forehead as if he didn't want the sun in his eyes while he was figuring on such a weighty problem.

"I'd have to study about it, Homer," he said. "There's some things I'd have to know. Was it an old mouse or a young un?"

"Medium-aged," said Homer. "This one was."

"A middle-aged mouse," said Jess. "Country mouse or city mouse?"

"City mouse."

"Well," said Jess, "my guess is . . . if properly encouraged . . . it could."

"Yes, sir," said Homer, his eyes sparkling. "That's right. It can."

"Why, Homer," Jess said, "thee's told me something I didn't know. I'll go to bed tonight a smarter man for having met thee." . . .

One Saturday . . . Jess took a turn about the house after dinner to inspect the early blooms. He was standing, sniffing and admiring in front of Eliza's bed of lilies-of-the-valley now almost in full flower, when Homer, barefoot and silent, joined him. . . .

"Well, Homer," he said, "if stars were sweet they'd be lilies-of-the-valley. If these lilies lit up after dark they'd be stars."

Jess smiled down on the boy, waiting to hear what lilies-of-the-valley were to Homer, to be given the glimpse he had come to value, of the world seen through a pair of eyes somewhat less rusty from use than his own. But Homer said nothing, only stood very still, drawing deep breaths, his pale lips unsmiling, as if a bed of lilies were a serious matter, and the pulse in his throat beating as if they were exciting too.

Jess noted that the boy had grown peakeder and thought that he had been mistaken, believing, as he had, that spring and sunlight would set whatever ailed him to rights.

"Homer," he asked, "has thee had thy sulphur and molasses yet this spring?"

Homer did not reply but dropping to his knees began to fill his hands with lilies. He had a half dozen before Jess could stop him.

"Homer," he said sternly, "thee give me those blossoms."

Homer stood up and without a word laid them in Jess's hands.

"Why, Homer," Jess said, "thee surprises me. I wouldn't pick these lilies myself. They belong to Eliza and she picks a few only now and then to scent the rooms. And here thee comes without so much as a by-thy-leave and falls to picking as if thee's the owner. I'm taken aback and ashamed, Homer, to see thee so unmannerly."

Still Homer did not say a word, only reached out one finger to touch the flowers Jess held, as if saying good-bye to them, then ran off toward the barn, hunting, Jess supposed, the new kittens. When he came back to the house he was as cheerful as if nothing had happened. He sat at the kitchen table, ate a thick slice of Eliza's good custard pie, and if he noticed the six lilies-of-the-valley which now stood in a cut glass bowl on the center of the table, he didn't show it.

But Jess noticed them. After Homer had left, the six lilies propped up by cut glass and kept moderately alive by water troubled him. . . . He didn't doubt he'd done the right thing . . . still, doing the right thing shouldn't leave such an ache under his breastbone . . . ; when he rose, finally . . . he was somewhat easier in his mind, he had come to a decision.

The weather next morning had changed, however, and for the better part of a week Jess was housebound. . . .

When the sun had somewhat dried the ground underfoot, Jess put on coat and hat, picked the few lilies the storm had spared—not many more than Homer himself had first gathered—and set off with them toward the Perkinses. . . .

The lilies warmed both by the sun and his own clasping hand were as sweetly scented as if they had never felt wind or hail and Jess thinking of the pleasure he would have putting them in Homer's hand was very easy in his heart.

Still, he was neither surprised nor, for the moment, touched by sorrow at the concourse, the gathering of rigs and people he saw beneath the pines and in front of the small, white house, nor did he for a moment doubt the meaning of their gathering. His feet, of themselves it seemed, continued his forward motion, while his mind in quiet lucidity stood apart and saw himself travel toward that meaning: saw, it seemed, this old man start eighty years before a journey destined to proceed from that branch at Colerain, through duck ponds, courting, the substance of father and householder, to mount at last this particular small rise on a spring day carrying lilies which would be heaped with other flowers on a trestle in a neighbor's front yard and there soften, but not hide what that trestle had been set up to bear.

His feet carried him onward . . . this is the time, the hour, the minute thee has walked toward, he told himself—and it seemed to him then that neither marrying nor praying, worshiping nor begetting had held for him such significance, and that he either now saw or forever missed such meaning as his eighty years on earth might have. Set on earth . . . believing this or that to be thy call, thy duty. Hunting thy apportioned way. Thinking in terms of Jess Birdwell, husband, countryman, churchman . . . all maybe wrong. Maybe no more than this . . . this maybe the end-all, and meaning, if any, here in climbing this hill with storm-damaged flowers for a small boy's funeral . . . and to lay them there with the others, likewise storm-damaged, concluding for the time, nothing . . . listening . . . asking.

There was no need for any words of explanation, he could have said them all himself, turned and told the others: Homer's heart had finished beating . . . in his small room he had lain as if asleep, smiling and with a look of listening. Jess wasn't sorrowing for Homer. Homer, he didn't misdoubt, had seen more of the world in his twelve years than this whole gathering lumped together, their experiences of seeing, hearing, wondering, bound together in a bundle and counted as that of one. He didn't sorrow for Homer, having some idea, as he did, of the way this world would have used him . . . how people like himself, with the best of intentions . . . trying to do their duty, merely . . . would have hurt and hampered him at every turn.

He didn't sorrow for himself, even—for the mischance at the end, yes—but he rejoiced that for a short time when all of his own young people were gone, a boy who had no father had been a son to him . . . and now he too was gone. He stood with the others and heard the familiar words . . . "Let not your hearts be troubled . . . in my Father's house are many mansions . . . I go to prepare a place for you."

The spring sun was setting when he turned homeward, his feet still taking care of his going while the whole longer journeying of his life busied his mind. Jess didn't sorrow for himself, nor for Homer . . . still he knew there were words he had misused, questions he had never asked, answers he had missed and he felt heavy with searching.

He sat in the kitchen beside the table where the six lilies, now much yellowed, still stood and he spoke to Eliza of the afternoon, his walk and his thoughts. They sat there together until dark had come, and Eliza had lit a lamp and set forth some food. Then while he ate and drank, the meaning he had searched for that afternoon, and maybe his whole life, seemed to shape itself. He took a last bite of bread, a last sup of tea.

"Eliza," he said, "I'm eighty years old. All my life I've been trying one way or another to do people good. Whether that was right or not, I don't know, but it comes over me now that I'm excused from all that. I loved Homer, but I tried to do him good . . . the way I see it now, that was wrong, that was where I's led astray. From now on, Eliza, I don't figure there's a thing asked of me but to love my fellowmen."

He got up from the table and went to the window. The earlier resplendence of the sky had faded, leaving only a small finger-shaped stretch of yellow light to show where the sun had been and where it had set. But the coming of dark had never dispirited Jess, and he spoke now with cheerfulness. "No, Eliza," he said, "as far as I can see, there's not another thing asked of me, from this day forward." «

CHAPTER SIX

Remembering Services

Wʜᴇɴ ᴏᴜʀ ᴄʜɪʟᴅʀᴇɴ were seven and eleven, we moved to a community where we did not know a single person. Those were lonesome days. The man in the bank where we paid the rent suggested we visit his church; he and his wife even went the second mile and on Sunday drove us to the Methodist church.

That was in 1938, but I still remember the sermon text: "What doth the Lord require of thee, but to do justly, and to love mercy, and to walk humbly with thy God?" The minister, W. Emory Hartman, spoke out for justice for all people. He put first things first.

A good sermon, however, does not overcome homesickness. We struggled through each day, just waiting to take the train back to grandparents, friends, playmates. Would Christmas never come? The morning we were to start, our son woke up with mumps. Gloom almost encompassed us. But a tree was bought and trimmed; the biggest turkey yet was stuffed and roasted; and the Christmas books were being read aloud, when Dr. and Mrs. Hartman came to call. They not only preached but practiced kindness.

Our friendship developed through the years as did my education in what constitutes the good life. Moreover from this family I continued to learn how to accept death without fear—for oneself and for those most dearly loved.

When the Hartmans' daughter died they sent us a copy of the memorial service.

A DOOR AJAR

» We are met here to remember Carolyn Hartman Kelly, affectionately known to us as Lyn. In a very fine way she wanted us to remember her even as our Lord wished to be remembered when he broke bread and took the cup, and there is a sacramental quality in what we do here because she lived and died close to her Lord and her God.

Well, what to say about one so fine, so splendid in mind and body and in spirit? Whatever we say, it will not be enough; nor can we say it all. Those who knew and loved her best confess to a mystery here. Her truth, the truth she lived by, the truth that was in her, was beyond definition. It was of the quality and mystery of God. It dwelt in her.

"Bless the Lord, O my soul; and all that is within me, bless his holy name!" This was, or so it seemed to me and to many others, her heart's desire, her constant prayer. She knew prayer, that elemental, natural response of the human spirit to the eternal God that dwells in the amazing inner sanctuary of the soul. This sanctuary she entered frequently. With it she was well acquainted, and from it she came renewed and strengthened. I know that she would have been surprised to discover that we thought this of her. She would have smiled and laughed heartily, not in derision, but with wonder and appreciation at this thing that happens to people who respond to the God that is within them, and regard their bodies as temples of the living God. A physicist said . . . that when a person dies it is like a whole universe exploding—so vast, so intricate, so beyond our understanding is the body, the mind, the spirit, the personality of a man or a woman. And so it is.

We study the cellular structure of the body and come away so baffled. The mind that seeks to fathom the universe turns upon itself and declares, "Thou art wonderfully and fearfully made"; and the heart with its loves and its hurts, its desires, its insights, its disappointments, its affections, its searching and questions, who can measure? Age after age men seek to understand this. There is not time enough to figure it all out, or to write all the psalms men would write, or to express their prayers adequately, or to describe their theologies, or even to sing their doxologies.

But because God has called men sons and daughters, they have their intimations of a relationship with the eternal God, and they come to know an eternal quality in their own lives. After all, it took a psalmist to say:

When I look at thy heavens, the work of thy fingers,
the moon and the stars which thou hast established;

what is man that thou art mindful of him,
and the son of man that thou dost care for him?

Yet thou hast made him little less than God,
and dost crown him with glory and honor.

Mrs. Kelly felt this about the world and her place in it. She was in love with life. She fought fiercely and gallantly to live. She did not want to die so young. Every resource of medical knowledge was sought and used to stem the disease which threatened her life and her hope, as was every resource of faith and prayer known to her and to her church and to her loved ones. Beloved friends in the Iona communities across the seas, beloved friends in this church, in our church at Storrs [Connecticut], and a host of persons scattered far and wide prayed that if it were possible this cup might pass from her. But this is not to say that she feared death or would not accept it when it came. She believed and had learned to pray (and this I know as one of her pastors), "Not my will but thine, O Lord, be done." We who knew her gained so much from her. She and her husband have helped in so many ways with the problem that few in our time have learned to master and with which so much help is needed. They had a terrible load to carry and they gave others an opportunity to share it with them. Here the church of Christ has become alive and real to a multitude of people. It was the Christ who said, "Bear one another's burdens."

"What can we do to help?" How many times during this past year I have heard people ask that question. How many times it has been asked here in this church and in this community. It is blessed to give, as our Lord said, but it is also blessed to receive. They received, with a graciousness that repaid ten times over all who offered help.

The Kellys talked openly of the cancer that invaded the body. They helped others to lift that word out of the taboo and the frightening shadows in which it has been and is held by so many. They shed light where light desperately needs to shine. Their friends started a Carolyn Hartman Kelly cancer fund to fight this insidious disease.

Mrs. Kelly was a young minister's wife and she was schooled for this position in the best school of all, the parsonage. No one could have been better qualified. She had learned the subtle requirements. She possessed an inquisitive mind, a heroic spirit, a love for people, and a generous nature. These things endeared her to little children, high school young people, university students, college professors, people in every walk and class of life, old and young alike. I have seen this happen to a remarkable degree in the few short months she was with us.

She loved the earth and the fullness thereof, flowers and grass, birds, animals; these things were dear to her life.

The reach of her mind was wide. New ideas thrilled her. Music, poetry, and biography of great and good men were her study and delight. But fun, play, laughter, and humor all were a part of her.

A close friend and classmate of her husband wrote him yesterday: "Someone has said that a saint is a person who makes it easier for you to believe in God. Lyn's illness and death have been terribly hard for us; I can only imagine what they've done to you and your families but through them you two have become something in my life and I'm sure in many more lives than you'll ever realize, and so my sorrow is mixed with thanksgiving and joy."

This is true of all of us. Shock sometimes angers, hurts, and saddens. But in a very wonderful way all of us are lifted up somehow, strengthened and gladdened because God has let one of his most beautiful creations touch our lives. As we look back upon the Christian faith that was Lyn Kelly's, many of us will rightly affirm that death itself to her was but the wider opening of the door that had been opening more and more through all her life and never was shut and never shall be shut. She left the door ajar for you and me. Looking after her we see the glory shining through the cleft. "And I heard a great voice out of heaven saying, Behold, the tabernacle of God is with men, and he will dwell with them, and they shall be his people, and God himself shall be with them, and be their God. And God shall wipe away all tears from their eyes; and there shall be no more death, neither sorrow, nor crying, neither shall there be any more pain: for the former things are passed away."

. . .

» *Prayer:* Our Father, we praise thee that we cannot think of Carolyn's death without looking beyond it. We are upheld by the assurance that in her passing from us there is no finality, but the sure promise of a fresh beginning, the doorway into a larger life of perfect peace and rest with thee. We praise thee for the knowledge in Christ that death is not the destruction of life but the expansion of life; that it cannot take us out of thy hands or separate us from thy love. Help us, dear God, never to forget that we are the children of eternal love, that love takes care of her own, and that underneath are the everlasting arms.

Most gracious God, we rejoice in all of the good things that have come to us through Carolyn's life. We bless thee for all those qualities her life showed that made others love her. For the love which she so freely gave and modestly received; for her youth and beauty, for her fine mind and enthusiasm for learning; for her sparkling humor, O God, we thank thee.

For her love of the out-of-doors, of mountains and of small creatures; for her love of all beauty, of music, of line and form and rhythm, O God, we thank thee. For her great interest in people and her deep love for them; for her compassion and concern, her honesty and forthrightness, her gentleness and humility, her quiet dignity, O God, we bless thee. For the magnificent courage that she wore as a mantle in the long months of illness and pain, O God, we praise thee. But most of all we thank thee for her deep and abiding trust in thee, for her devotion to Jesus Christ and his church, for the radiance of faith that shone through her and touched all around her with its glow. . . .

Finally, dear God, through our memory of Carolyn, this day, teach us to live as those who are prepared to die, and when thy summons comes to us, soon or late, O God, teach us to die as those who are prepared to go on living in thine eternal kingdom. Whether living or dying, nothing shall separate us from thy great redeeming love as revealed in Jesus Christ our Lord and Savior. AMEN.

The Lord bless you and keep you. The Lord make his face

to shine upon you, and be gracious to you. The Lord lift up the light of his countenance upon you, and give you peace and comfort and strength of mind and heart to continue to live on in his service.

Now he who is able to keep you from falling, and to present you faultless before his presence with exceeding joy, the only wise God our Father, keep your minds and your hearts today and forever. AMEN. «

MIRACULOUS CHRISTMAS TO YOU!

Six months after Carolyn's death, her father wrote this message to his congregation:

» The re-creation year after year of the Christmas state of mind in the consciousness of millions of people is a miracle of spiritual transformation.

For Christmas breaks down the harsh barriers in our hearts. Christmas softens us, sweetens us, removes the rigid self-righteousness and punctures our pretensions. Christmas makes us humble and grateful for life and its goodness, for friends and their understanding, for the fellowship of good people, who hold us up. Christmas gets us to thinking of others—not just our families, our set, our crowd, our church, but about those brothers who are hungry and homeless and afraid.

But the supreme miracle is that Christmas encourages us to become nobler than we are. It helps us to believe that tomorrow we can be better than we are today. For the Christ of Christmas is the great inspirer of men. Said he, "I, if I be lifted up from the earth, will draw all men unto myself."

So my wish is that we may have a miraculous Christmas, experiencing in our own lives the fulfillment of the promise: "If anyone is in Christ, he is a new creation; the old has passed away, behold, the new has come." «

A HUMBLE AND GRATEFUL REJOICING

Three years after his daughter's death a memorial service was held for Dr. Hartman; it was my great privilege to be present. I have never been so uplifted as I was then by that worshiping congregation met together to give thanks for the leadership and friendship of so rare a soul. The beautiful old hymns of faith were sung triumphantly by all present—personal friends, members of the church, members of his own family.

In songs of faith and hope, in prayers of adoration and thanksgiving, all present were witnessing to the truth that death cannot kill that which never dies, for the things of the spirit are eternal.

We sang "Still, still with thee, when purple morning breaketh, when the bird waketh, and the shadows flee," and we sang Emory Hartman's favorite Whittier hymn:

> I know not what the future hath
> Of marvel or surprise,
> Assured alone that life and death
> His mercy underlies.
>
> And if my heart and flesh are weak
> To bear an untried pain,
> The bruisèd reed he will not break,
> But strengthen and sustain.
>
> And thou, O Lord, by whom are seen
> Thy creatures as they be,
> Forgive me if too close I lean
> My human heart on thee!
>
> And so beside the silent sea
> I wait the muffled oar;
> No harm from him can come to me
> On ocean or on shore.

I know not where his islands lift
Their fronded palms in air;
I only know I cannot drift
Beyond his love and care.

And we honored his memory by praying the prayer he loved, being fully aware that love sustained him to the end.

Teach me to love thee as thine angels love,
One holy passion filling all my frame;
The baptism of the heaven-descended Dove,
My heart an altar, and thy love the flame.

AMEN.

A SHEAF OF CHRISTMAS MEMORIES

How great a grief to watch a brilliant college student go down to the gates of death! In a letter his mother wrote: "We are finding that the road to inner peace and confidence is long and hard. The mind knows, but the bereft heart is slow to accept, especially in the case of a beloved child with the promise of so rich and significant a life ahead of him hastening so abruptly out of this world. But we are earth-centered creatures and cannot understand those 'miracles of the spirit' of which George Fox wrote."

Perhaps it was a miracle of grace that prompted these parents to write down and then share their memories of Christmas; perhaps in the remembering there was a measure of healing.

» In hearts that keep Christmas, the season is a time of memories, added to and hallowed, year by year—memories of childish joy and parental love, of quiet wonder and worship, of warm fires and savory smells and homecomings, of gaiety and goodwill.

This Christmas season . . . we are especially remembering Jim, and his sensitivity and insight through which we caught glimpses of the true meaning of Christmas.

We remember him, his first three Christmases, enthralled with the lights on our tree, and on trees in neighboring courtyards of Chicago, where we then lived. His childish wonder at the lights, glowing suddenly in the darkness where no lights had shone before, became then, and has remained for us, the symbolic way to Christmas.

We remember the season he was five. Days before Christmas we put up the crèche, placing most of the traditional figures in a studied arrangement at some distance from the stable. Coming into the room later, we found Jimmy herding together sheep and shepherds, camels and wisemen, close against the stable door. "They wanted to see the baby Jesus," he explained. "They couldn't see him when they were standing out in the field like that."

We remember the season he was six. It had been our custom each year to trim our tree with all the old, treasured ornaments collected over the years and carefully packed away at the end of each season. But that year we had tried something different, and our tree, we thought, looked regally splendid in its adornment of dozens of newly purchased lustrous purple balls. One afternoon we returned home from an errand to find Jimmy perched on the kitchen stool beside the tree, and, hung on the branches, along with the purple balls, all the old beloved ornaments around which sentiment had gathered—tinkly bells and glass balls of many colors and sizes; metal icicles; ragged stars; china toadstools; three small, dirty Santa Clauses; a disheveled angel; a little Eskimo on broken skis; and crumpled paper chains. "Didn't you think the tree pretty as it was?" we asked. "You forgot these things," he said.

We remember the season he was twelve. Wearing a borrowed terry-cloth bathrobe too big for him, and a Roman striped scarf about his head, he played the part of a shepherd boy in the school play. During the whole of that Christmas season he had to be reminded of matters at hand because his ears were ringing with strange, sweet music borne on the wind, and he was hurrying into Bethlehem to see what wonder had befallen in a stable.

We remember especially Jim's last Christmas with us, before his death in February of this year. On the day before Christmas he lay ill, watching as we busily wrapped gifts. "All these *things* at Christmas time!" he mused. "Don't they depress you? Why don't we *do* for people instead?"

In hearts that keep Christmas, the season is a time of memories, added to and hallowed, year by year. In sharing these memories with you, we hope your Christmas will be gracious with memories of your own—sweet, poignant, and tender. «

AND GLADLY DIE

From the beginning of the Religious Society of Friends in the seventeenth century, the people called Quakers have had a concern for simplicity in all things regarding their dead. The present-day practice, in general, is to hold a memorial service several days after burial or cremation; this follows the pattern of the regular Sunday meeting for worship. The family and friends and members gather in the quiet meetinghouse and sit in silent prayer. After a time usually several of the Friends present will rise and speak of the life of the one they have come to remember, or quote a passage from scripture, or share some bit of poetry. At the service of one of our beloved friends, my husband quoted Robert Louis Stevenson's "Requiem,"

Under the wide and starry sky,
Dig the grave and let me lie.
Glad did I live and gladly die,
And I laid me down with a will.

This be the verse you grave for me:
Here he lies where he longed to be;
Home is the sailor, home from the sea,
And the hunter home from the hill.

But there is no rule. On another occasion, that I remember well, the closed coffin was present in the meetinghouse while Friends gathered to worship and give thanks. Later this prayer was spoken by an Episcopalian for her Quaker friend at the graveside:

» O Father, almighty, all-merciful, all-loving, unto whom all hearts are open, all desires known, and from whom no secrets are hid, we thank thee for all the goodness which has passed from the life of this thy servant into the life of others and has left the world richer for her presence. For a life's task faithfully and honorably discharged; for good humor and gracious affection and kindly generosity; for sadness met with surrender, and weakness endured without defeat. Give us eyes to see and hearts to feel the undefeated courage, the invincible faith, the unconquerable love which thou hast revealed to us in this triumphant spirit.

Fill our hearts with praise and gratitude for her unshaken conviction that no distress, suffering, or perplexity, neither death, nor things present nor things to come, could separate us from the love of God which she had seen in Christ Jesus our Lord. Let the light which we beheld in her never forsake us. Grant to us, in any experience which may come to us, her faith, her courage, her hope, her integrity, her capacity for caring, and bless us with an everabiding sense of her presence. We entrust her to thy care, our Father, knowing that thou who art Love art doing for her better things than we can desire or pray for. AMEN. «

ART FOR A PURPOSE

Grief can enlarge the hearts of those who are nearest and dearest, and beyond the inner circle of family and friends remembering services—whether spoken in churches or written at Christmas—can uplift the spirits of all who are touched. Everyone to some degree is quickened in sensitivity by the death of a truly good person. But for most of us our areas of awareness, of caring, are circumscribed.

Kathe Kollwitz, whose son was killed in World War II, has used her artistic gift to awaken people to the evils of war. She is famous for her drawings of mothers and children, especially the heartbroken mothers and underfed children of the war years. "When [this German artist] had to work on a placard against war for the International Trade Union Organization, she regarded it as a 'task which gives me great pleasure. . . . When I know that I am working with an international community against war I have a sense of warm, intense satisfaction. . . . I can understand that my art has a purpose.' "

GO DOWN, DEATH

During the eight years that I led a poetry club at the Philadelphia Center for Older People, many parties were given for us in beautiful homes. After a bountiful and delicious luncheon the program went on as usual with everyone present reading or reciting a poem.

The members will never forget the day we were entertained at the John Woolman Memorial in Mount Holly, New Jersey. The Presbyterian minister, invited to participate in food and fellowship, read aloud "Go Down, Death."

> Weep not, weep not,
> She is not dead;
> She's resting in the bosom of Jesus.
> Heartbroken husband—weep no more;
> Grief-stricken son—weep no more;
> Left-lonesome daughter—weep no more;
> She's only just gone home.
>
> Day before yesterday morning,
> God was looking down from his great, high heaven,
> Looking down on all his children,
> And his eye fell on Sister Caroline,
> Tossing on her bed of pain,
> And God's big heart was touched with pity,
> With the everlasting pity.
>
> And God sat back on his throne,
> And he commanded that tall, bright angel standing
>   at his right hand:
> Call me Death!
> And that tall, bright angel cried in a voice
> That broke like a clap of thunder:
> Call Death!—Call Death!
> And the echo sounded down the streets of heaven
> Till it reached away back to that shadowy place,
> Where Death waits with his pale, white horses.
>
> And Death heard the summons,
> And he leaped on his fastest horse,
> Pale as a sheet in the moonlight,
> Up the golden street Death galloped,

And the hoofs of his horse struck fire from the gold,
But they didn't make no sound.
Up Death rode to the Great White Throne,
And waited for God's command.

And God said: Go down, Death, go down,
Go down to Savannah, Georgia,
Down in Yamarcraw,
And find Sister Caroline.
She's borne the burden and heat of the day,
She's labored long in my vineyard,
And she's tired—
She's weary—
Go down, Death, and bring her to me.

And Death didn't say a word,
But he loosed the reins on his pale, white horse,
And he clamped the spurs to his bloodless sides,
And out and down he rode,
Through heaven's pearly gates,
Past suns and moons and stars;
On Death rode,
And the foam from his horse was like a comet in
    the sky;
On Death rode,
Leaving the lightning's flash behind;
Straight on down he came.

While we were watching round her bed,
She turned her eyes and looked away,
She saw what we couldn't see;
She saw Old Death. She saw Old Death,
Coming like a falling star.
But Death didn't frighten Sister Caroline;
He looked to her like a welcome friend.

And she whispered to us: I'm going home,
And she smiled and closed her eyes.

And Death took her up like a baby,
And she lay in his icy arms,
But she didn't feel no chill.
And Death began to ride again—
Up beyond the evening star,
Out beyond the morning star,
Into the glittering light of glory,
On to the Great White Throne.
And there he laid Sister Caroline
On the loving breast of Jesus.

And Jesus took his own hand and wiped away her
   tears,
And he smoothed the furrows from her face,
And the angels sang a little song,
And Jesus rocked her in his arms,
And kept a-saying: Take your rest,
Take your rest, take your rest.

Weep not—weep not,
She is not dead;
She's resting in the bosom of Jesus.

                                        —James Weldon Johnson

CHAPTER SEVEN

Being Companioned

Grow strong, my comrade, . . . that you may stand
Unshaken when I fall; that I may know
The shattered fragments of my song will come
At last to finer melody in you;
That I may tell my heart that you begin
Where passing I leave off, and fathom more.

—Will Durant

BLESSINGS ON ALL those rare souls who are able to speak about the things that really matter—marrying and dying and God. How should we ever learn to run the race that is set before us, if it were not for the cloud of witnesses who have shown the way?

BEYOND MY DREAM

In our meditation group we talked together of death and sorrow, of how much simpler it is to face death for ourselves than to be the one left sorrowing. We grieve for our own loneliness, our desolation on the journey we must face bereft of a beloved companion.

And then a new member spoke out, "But there is a sense of being companioned that can come." We must have looked at her wide-eyed. "Oh, nothing supernatural, not voices, but a sense of no longer being alone."

We were told that after her husband's death she was inconsolable. They both had been teachers of English and had had no children, so they had lived for their pupils, their books, and for each other. They were kindred spirits as well as lovers. During the early weeks of grief a friend called and in the conversation advised her to get a large notebook and write in it each day. But Carmen Blanc insisted that she was not one to make a diary of her innermost feelings. The friend went on to suggest it need not be an account of her intimate thoughts but a record of the words that spoke to her condition as she reread the books beloved by both husband and wife.

She purchased a five-year diary and began to cull lovely poignant thoughts, prayers, excerpts from letters, snatches of conversation, and everything which radiated hope. A friend christened this bulging notebook her "Star Points," as indeed it came to be. One day a line leaped out at her from a poem by Sara Teasdale: "If I could make a single song . . ." and she thought, I can, I can. She continued to read, now going far and wide until the facets of her husband's character finally stood revealed through the authors he so loved—Chaucer, Plato, Shakespeare, Browning, Schweitzer, Stevenson, Yeats, Blake, Emerson, Masefield, Keats, Rodin, Picasso, Pater, Whitehead, Matthew Arnold, Edith Hamilton. The work completed, she then hand-lettered the manuscript which a friend beautifully bound in black leather. Here was Robert E. Blanc, alive and speaking in the poetry and prose.

The little book has been printed for friends. Its title is *Beyond My Dream,* from Euripides:

O great in our dull world of clay,
And great in heaven's undying gleam,
Pallas, thy bidding we obey:
And bless thee, for mine ears have heard
The joy and wonder of a word
Beyond my dream, beyond my dream.

In the introduction Mrs. Blanc pays tribute to her husband:

» For my husband great books held the answers and the questions of life. He lived in the rarefied atmosphere of profound thoughts and the moving beauty of splendid, ringing words. This is the reason for the plan of so slender an offering. Let the words of the great writers he loved catch the gleaming facets of his gentle and living soul, his universal, rapier-like mind.

Such fare was his daily meat: these ways we walked together. The really great joy I have had in doing this work of love was when his books were in my hands and I explored again and again the pages where he had led me. He leads me still. This I know as my thoughts go ever inward. These few pages are necessarily incomplete, for I could never capture all of Robert who was so completely civilized a man. I hope, however, something of his wide humanity and of his truest and best emerges from them.

Some people it is not well for the world to lose, although these shining ones can remain with us if we but take off our shoes. They live in the deep core of our being and also in the great reservoir of beauty and wisdom and culture on which we all draw for our daily bread. Perhaps a thought, generated here in contemplation of Robert, will wing its way onward to pause in the hearts of others and there reveal everwidening areas for meditation. That is my simple hope, and this is my tribute to the enchantment which was our marriage, and to what marriage can be when it is star-caught. «

» "When grief loses itself in beauty, eternity is born." Life at its highest level I conceive of as struggle against spiritual apathy. Personal grief, I have found, must lose itself in the larger patterns of the world's pain. Beauty is God's gift upon the heart, and eternity is that pulsing, encompassing moment—the present.

Many years ago a shattering blow fell upon the shoulders of a gifted friend, and the small world in which we moved was dissolved in heartbreak. . . .

Grief into beauty! "Yet man is born unto trouble as the sparks fly upward," and the bonds of sorrow are the heritage of our common humanity. The first moment of personal heartbreak seems too terrible to be borne. Grief envelopes, utter lostness is in the heart, wild questions are upon the lips. Why is this sorrow mine? Why do the innocent suffer? Why must the good and the beautiful be senselessly hurt? Why are those so needed taken from us? Why, why, why?

At this point there seems nothing to live for. The world is dissolved about us, and we grope blindly for a way. We move forward day by day, how, we do not know. Naught but God's grace saves us until we can learn to forgive ourselves. This is what someone wise calls the first creative act of "grief's slow wisdom." We face our own limitations and understand with complete surety that everything we long for of endurance or peace or happiness comes to us only through his touch upon our souls. . . .

I turned to those artists who release the godhead of their genius in stone and color and soaring space. I turned to the makers of music and to beauty everywhere. . . . Above all else I found courage in "the jeweled cup" of Shakespeare and in the sweep of the Greek tragic poets. . . .

The alchemy of beauty does change sorrow, lifting and bearing it aloft to cleanse and strengthen the human heart. Beauty is a religious experience, and suffering is a beauty in itself, and a prayer. «

—Carmen Heath Blanc

MY WORLD WAS WRECKED

From her own sore loss Elizabeth Gray Vining tells how healing comes and companionship continues.

» When I was young I thought that beauty and courage and human love were the enduring values by which I could live. The beauty of nature, of an apple-green sky in a December twilight, of sunshafts through trees, of distant mountains, the beauty of words in poetry or fine prose, fed my spirit. Courage—even a little of it—enabled me to face the disappointments that come to all young writers and to weather the disasters of the Great Depression. Human love meant for me a circle of friends and family and, above all, my brilliant and adored husband, Morgan Vining.

In 1933 he was killed in an automobile accident and I was seriously injured myself. I had nine weeks in bed to contemplate the wreckage of my world. I realized then that beauty and courage and human love, though indispensable, were not enough. During a long winter I sought desperately for the rock of truth on which to build my life anew and found it in the silent worship of the Quaker meeting. In discovering there the love of God, I found the love of neighbor infinitely widened and deepened. The realization that there is a spark of the divine in every human soul draws together people of all races, all creeds, all nations, all classes. This is why war is evil, and social injustice unendurable, why religion is incomplete without service. . . .

I have come to understand that we see only a small part of the whole pattern of existence. Sorrow and suffering give opportunities for growth. Disappointment often opens doors to wider fields. The tragedy of death, as someone wiser than I has said, is separation, but even separation may not be permanent. The sense of continuing companionship with those who have gone beyond the horizon which comes to me occasionally makes me confident that someday we shall see beyond the mystery which now we must accept. Often it seems that those who have most to give to the world are the very ones who are taken from it in the flower of their youth and vigor. It is hard to understand why this should be so, unless—and this I believe to be true—they have done whatever it was they had to do here, have fulfilled their secret contract with this world, and have been released for more important work elsewhere. «

» There have been times, when I was alone in a scene of great natural beauty, when I have been aware of the presence of one whom I loved and could not see. The joy of the moment and the lasting, vivid quality of the memory seem to speak for its authenticity. . . .

> I was alone on that road.
> Clouds moved swiftly overhead,
> And a light as clear as water
> Lay on the horizon. It was May,
> The hawthorn white with bloom,
> Saint Mary's lace wincing in the wind
> Beside the road. A lapwing cried,
> Soaring and dipping above the field
> Where rabbits huddled in circles,
> Brown and bowed their small bodies.

Drenched by sudden rain that swept
Like dim curtains blowing,
I walked toward Ewelme, where
Chaucer's son lay buried,
Where in five centuries the feet of old men
Have hollowed the stone steps between
The almshouse and the church.

I walked alone, wind-buffeted
Feeling the chill fingers of rain
Touch my face, tasting the rain
On my lips, hearing the lapwing's cry,
Smelling the wet, warm earth,
Seeing the storm move toward the world's edge
And the pale sun run after it.
I walked alone in that wide country.

Yet not alone. Oh, not alone!
And I, who hold the dead do not
Return to the living, being free,
Not hovering nostalgic over old scenes,
Not bound even by old loves,
I sang aloud on the empty road,
Exulting, rich at heart, because
You walked there with me. «

—Elizabeth Gray Vining

SEEK AND YE SHALL FIND

In his spiritual autobiography, *The Road Home,*
James McBride Dabbs writes:

» Sixteen days after Jessie's death, I had an experience
so strange, yet so simple, that it is difficult to record. In spite
of my feeling of kinship with the universe, in spite of the
assurance, however brief, that our ideals have objective

existence, Jessie was still lost. Turn where I would, I could not find her. On this particular evening, writing to a friend, I said, "We whom she loved must keep her memory in our hearts. Perhaps some day I shall find where she is." Soon afterward I went to bed; and in a few minutes, without warning, and with no surprise, I realized that she was with me, a warm and living presence, all about me and all within me. I had a mental image of her then, asleep and smiling in a still room, and the room was myself. I hugged myself and smiled too, for the most part in happiness, slightly, however, in a pure amusement that this should have happened to me. Then, more peacefully than in years, I fell asleep. After two long weeks I had found her, and should never have to look any farther, questioning futilely her empty room and all the vacant air. Like its rightful owner, she had entered my heart and, unafraid, was sleeping.

When I awoke the next morning this new peace and happiness was still with me, and though it has never since been so luminous as it was at first, it has never really left me. Never since then have I turned to the empty air to ask where she was. Always there has been something with me, even within my body, like another self. My deepest desire for a long time was to realize more clearly this presence.

What happened? How do I know? I do know this: I entered a life beyond my knowledge, beyond even my dreams, and completely satisfying; a life filled with peace. I did not know that two persons could really be one. If anyone had spoken earlier of such an experience, I should have smiled and said, "Well—well, I don't know what you're talking about." During Jessie's lifetime I had spent many months away from her: always she was somewhere out there, a thousand or three thousand miles away; I could remember her, imagine her, but she was she and I was I. Now, without effort on my part (for how could I strive for what I could

not imagine?) she had become I yet had remained herself,
I had become she yet had remained myself. I ask no one to
believe this: if you do not know it, it is absurd; if you do
know it, it is the deepest truth. . . .

Perhaps my vision of her was her victory over death. Perhaps my happiness at her coming was matched, and sur-
passed, by her own. My communion with her, though word-
less, is none the less communion. So perhaps is her communion with me.

But I am sure only of the experience itself. Of its causes,
its final meaning, I do not know, but wonder. Though I shall
not urge that anything that I did caused the experience, I do
wonder if my attitude did not make it possible. Should I
have found her again, rather should I have come to
know her in this new way, if I had been resigned,
apathetic; if I had said with a sigh, "God's will be done"? To
have done that would have been to make beauty and ugliness
indistinguishable, to smear my hand across my life and call
all parts of it equal. If I had done that, she might indeed
have died; for having denied, I should soon have forgotten
her essential loveliness. But I rebelled at the loss; not bitterly,
I think, but persistently. I accepted the fact of death without approving of it. So far as I could see, all things were not
for the best, for a flower had been crushed. There was the
perfume of her life, to be sure, but what of her own desire?
She had not wished to be crushed. I knew I had to accept
her death. She was gone. Nor would all my crying bring her
back. But I didn't have to say it was all for the best.

I wonder why men so often say this. It seems to me that
the chief reason is weakness or a sort of practicality, or both.
It takes strength to accept a fact while holding it unreason-
able; and it seems impractical to fight against what has already happened. I could imagine such a practical person

saying to me, "But what's the use? You cannot bring her back." ...

It is not wise to grieve too much for a lost body; but neither is it wise to tell ourselves that nothing has been lost. We must try first of all to be truthful; sincerity is the one thing that matters. ...

Certainly in my better moments I was not resigned. The way to heaven, I told myself, . . . is through a passionate love of earth. Only ask enough of earth; face life forever with the dreams of your youth; never lower your demands one jot. You may have what you ask for—if you ask for it, and ask for it, and ask for it! "Ask, and it shall be given you; seek, and ye shall find; knock, and it shall be opened unto you." ...

If I had become resigned, it was, I think, somewhat in the sense in which Albert Schweitzer uses the term. I had come to realize my dependence upon events quite beyond my control; but, having realized this dependence, I had come to a sense of spiritual independence. "Our dependence upon events is not absolute; it is qualified by our spiritual freedom. Therefore when we speak of resignation it is not sadness to which we refer, but the triumph of our will-to-live over whatever happens to us." Resigning our bodies to life—and death—we refuse to resign our spiritual life. The struggle is not relinquished but transferred to another plane.

Perhaps it was such a refusal that brought me a reward. I had hoped only to remember her. I had not really hoped, though I had passionately desired, to find her. And I hardly think I did. I think God sent her back to me as a gift. But *perhaps* I had made my life ready to receive her; perhaps she couldn't have entered if I hadn't opened the door. ...

This much is sure: by the grace of God, I had come at last to Easter. «

My mentor, Adelaide Blomberg, for twenty-seven years has made real to me the life of the spirit. Of all the many fine books she has put into my hands, the one that has helped me most is *Things That Matter* by Bishop Brent.

THINGS THAT MATTER

» My experience of the past twelve months and more has shown me that the valley of the shadow of death is a highly illumined valley and is more akin to a mountain-top which reveals long views and endless vistas, than it is to a place of gloom. It is not with any sense of fear, but with an extraordinary clearness in one's estimate of values that one views the world from the edge of the grave. During the period of my enforced idleness I have been trying to estimate persons and things from what seemed to me the extraordinary vantage ground on the borders of the world of eternity. . . .

In our materialistic age we are apt to attach too much importance to the gifts of comfort and competence for which most men strain themselves, but the life of prayer, if it is to be genuine and true, keeps the soul day by day in the clear sunlight of God's protecting love. Probably the greatest fear that most people have is of that plunge into the unknown (or dimly known) which comes through death. Shakespeare has never impressed me as being a devout man but he had a fine type of religion which crops out again and again in his dramas. Here . . . is what he says about the fear of death:

> Cowards die many times before their deaths;
> The valiant never taste of death but once.
> Of all the wonders that I yet have heard,
> It seems to me most strange that men should fear;
> Seeing that death, a necessary end,
> Will come when it will come.

·   ·   ·

Love is, in its supreme triumphs, volitional rather than emotional. It creates affinities out of antagonisms, presences out of absences, friends out of enemies. Herein it displays its magic power, and finds its secret rejoicings. . . . Friendship, though fostered by, is not dependent upon, automatic or sensory presence. Often it is deepened . . . by physical absence. . . .

I have the quiet consolation, steadily growing, that death is only an incident, and that its power has been so broken that it can do little else than create a momentary break in intercommunication. Love somehow becomes more of a steady flame through death. If we hold in our inmost hearts those who have already gone, and they in like manner hold us, death is already abolished. . . .

It is a fact of history that the greatest figures are not known until after they die—from Socrates to Christ, and from Christ to Lincoln. What is true of the greater is true of the lesser. . . .

Another towering fact is that mortality is our kindergarten experience, our earliest conscious knowledge of a life that is not only everlasting but, more mysterious and wonderful still, also eternal. Space and time are seeming tyrants but neither is to be feared for our immortality smiles at both as we begin to practice it here and await with reverent curiosity for the wonders that are hidden behind successive veils of experience of which death is the last. Of course no one can help the suffering which comes in bereavement. Indeed who would escape it if he could? It is the one means left to us by which to declare the reality and depth of our love for the one taken. Were there no pain it would mean there had been no love or little love. Go on unanxiously with the glad knowledge that you and yours are tied by a bond against which death is as powerless as is a cloud to extinguish the sun or a hammer to destroy a moonbeam.

In these later years I have come to view life as being in itself tragedy. There is no escape. If it does not come in one form it does in another. What then? Here Christ and Christianity come in—not as a consolation merely when we share the common lot, but as an armor and a transforming power which make us victorious in defeat and in all things super-conquerors. Love is invincible, whether it be God's love for us, or ours for him or for one another. . . .

The City that lieth foursquare is the home of an ordered society, big enough for redeemed mankind, for it is complete and whole with the completeness and holiness of God. The kingdom of God, noble phrase! is the measure of the City. The kingdom is so humble and lowly that it can be and is within us. It is so comprehensive that it can contain mankind, and yet there is room. . . .

We must not allow our contemplation of the complete order of the City that lieth foursquare to exclude our social whole on earth, for the link that binds the one to the other is organic, vital, and intimate. The "here" is the "there" in the process of becoming. All that vast multitude which composes the majority of the race from the beginning has been able to reach the goal only by the way we are now treading. . . . The deposit they left on earth is our chief asset. On it we build our own contribution. What direct efforts they are making for our edification and encouragement, to what extent an individual hand there touches a life here, does not appear. But the self-giving of the whole rushes earthward through generous arteries, and gives us nourishment and cheer. We are compassed about with a great cloud of witnesses—not idle observers but sympathetic brethren. «

Sources and Acknowledgments

[Continued from page 2]

Page 2—"Death is only an old door . . ." An anonymous bit of verse often used at funeral services by the author's father-in-law, Dr. Herbert E. Benton.

Page 12—"O world, thou choosest not the better part . . ." "O World" from *Poems* by George Santayana. Charles Scribner's Sons, 1901.

"Every one of us has an intimate, personal concern . . ." From "The Soul's Invincible Surmise," a sermon preached by Harry Emerson Fosdick at Riverside Church in New York City on April 16, 1933.

Page 16—"But this we know . . ." From "The Two Mysteries" by Mary Mapes Dodge.

"In times of joy . . ." "Song of Loved Things" by Elizabeth-Ellen Long in *Ladies' Home Journal*, February 1946. © 1946 by The Curtis Publishing Company.

Page 18—"Not yet—not yet! we cry . . ." From "Home for Christmas" by Marylu Terral Jeans. Reprinted by permission from the December, 1956, issue of *Good Housekeeping* Magazine. © 1956 by the Hearst Corporation.

"When a good man dies . . ." From *Holy Dying* by Jeremy Taylor.

"All who have meant good work . . ." From *Aes Triplex* by Robert Louis Stevenson.

Page 19—"Christ binds us all together . . ." Translated from *Hymne de l'Univers* by Pierre Teilhard de Chardin, p. 129.

"Father of all mercy . . ." "A Litany for Those Who Mourn." Used by permission of De Koven Foundation, Racine, Wisconsin.

Page 21—"The solemn fields breathe out to me . . ." "English Easter: 7 A.M." From the book *Immanence* by Evelyn Underhill, pp. 20-21. Published by E. P. Dutton & Co., Inc., and reprinted with their permission.

Page 22—"If you asked me . . ." Alan Paton in *The Writer Observed* by Harvey Breit, p. 92. The World Publishing Co., 1956. Copyright © 1956 by Harvey Breit.

Page 23—"My friend, your anxiety turned to fear . . ." Excerpts from *Cry, the Beloved Country* by Alan Paton, pp. 106-8, 222-23, (Copyright 1948 Alan Paton) are reprinted with the permission of Charles Scribner's Sons.

Page 25—"One of the best-known legends . . ." "The Road to Maturity" by Bradford Smith in *Friends Journal*, August 15, 1964.

Page 27—"If anyone had told me . . ." From "My Last Best Days on Earth" by Hazel Beck Andre in *Farm Journal*, July 1956. © 1956 by Farm Journal, Inc. Reprinted by special permission of *Farm Journal* and *The Reader's Digest*.

126 : A DOOR AJAR

Page 28—"I am content to leave all my dear ones . . ." From *A Diary of Private Prayer* by John Baillie, p. 27. Charles Scribner's Sons, 1949.

Page 30—"A young mother named Lucile Fray . . ." Condensed from "A Mother's Last Year" by Jhan and June Robbins. Reprinted from *Redbook Magazine*, March 1956.

Pages 37-38—"Copious scrawled notes . . ." and "The summer walks fast . . ." From *And a Time to Die* by Mark Pelgrin, edited by Sheila Moon and Elizabeth B. Howes. Routledge & Kegan Paul, Ltd., 1961. © Sheila Moon and Elizabeth B. Howes, 1961.

Page 44—"You were nine that summer . . ." Adapted from *The Story of Gabrielle* by Catherine Gabrielson. The World Publishing Co., 1956. © 1956 by Catherine Gabrielson.

Page 48—"The newspaper details of the loss . . ." From *A Gift of Janice* by Max Wylie. Copyright © 1964 by Max Wylie. Reprinted by permission of Doubleday & Co., Inc.

Page 51—"I often think of that genuine faith . . ." From *The New Testament in Modern English,* translated by J. B. Phillips, p. 456. © J. B. Phillips, 1958. Used by permission of The Macmillan Co.

Page 56—"Be still and cool . . ." and "Feeling light within . . ." From *The Quiet Eye: A Way of Looking at Pictures* by Sylvia Shaw Judson. Henry Regnery Co., 1954.

Page 57—"The growth-curve of the body . . ." Howard C. Collier in *The Choice Is Always Ours,* edited by Dorothy Berkley Phillips, p. 303. Copyright, 1948, by Dorothy B. Phillips. Reprinted with permission of Harper & Row, Publishers, Inc.

Page 59—"To see a world in a grain of sand . . ." From "Auguries of Innocence" by William Blake.

Page 60—"LONDON (AP)—Prof. L. Dudley Stamp . . ." From "Obituary Honors Wife of 39 Years" in *The New York Times,* September 23, 1962.

Page 61—"Multiple sclerosis first attacked . . ." From "Mrs. Allen Loses 26-Year MS Battle" in *The Houston Post,* June 25, 1964.

Page 63—"I was walking back . . ." From *Through the Valley of the Kwai* by Ernest Gordon, pp. 140-46. Copyright © 1962 by Ernest Gordon. Reprinted with permission of Harper & Row, Publishers, Inc.

Page 67—"You too, gentlemen of the jury . . ." *The Last Days of Socrates* by Plato, translated by Hugh Tredennick, p. 50. Penguin Books, Ltd., 1954.

Page 69—"Grow old along with me . . ." From "Rabbi Ben Ezra" by Robert Browning.

Page 73—"From the hospital . . ." From *The Negro Spiritual Speaks of Life and Death* by Howard Thurman, pp. 18-19, 24. Reprinted with permission of Harper & Row, Publishers, Inc.

Page 74—"Wade in the water . . ." From *Deep River* by Howard Thurman, pp. 90, 93-94. Copyright 1945, 1955 by Howard Thurman. Reprinted with permission of Harper & Row, Publishers, Inc.

Page 76—"They wanted the doctor . . ." and "I must confess . . ." From *A Doctor's Casebook in the Light of the Bible* by Paul Tournier, pp. 170-74. Copyright 1960 by Harper & Brothers. Reprinted with permission of Harper & Row, Publishers, Inc.

Page 78—"When a patient is dying . . ." From "Prescription for Dying," reprinted from *Time,* The Weekly Newsmagazine, April 2, 1951; copyright Time, Inc.

Page 79—"Does it mean death . . ." From "Should We Let Them Die?" by Vincent J. Collins, M.D., in *The Saturday Evening Post,* May 26, 1962.

Page 82—"The Most Rev. Fulton J. Sheen . . ." From "No Moral Need to Extend Hopeless Lives, AMA Told" by Gary Brooten in *The Philadelphia Inquirer,* June 17, 1963.

Page 85—"We suggest the consideration . . ." Condensed from the charter of the Indianapolis Memorial Society.

Page 87—"Wilfreda Grayson: Of course she gives . . ." From *The River Garden of Pure Repose* by Grace M. Boynton. Copyright 1952 by Grace M. Boynton. Used by permission of McGraw-Hill Book Company.

Page 90—"When Jess was eighty . . ." Copyright, 1945, by Jessamyn West. Abridged from her volume *The Friendly Persuasion* by permission of Harcourt, Brace & World, Inc.

Page 97—"We are met here to remember . . ." From a memorial address by the Rev. J. Garland Waggoner of Storrs, Conn.

Page 100—"Prayer: Our Father . . ." From a prayer by the Rev. Irvin G. Thursby of Milford, Conn.

Page 103—"Still, still with thee . . ." From "Still, Still with Thee" by Harriet Beecher Stowe.

"I know not what the future hath . . ." From "The Eternal Goodness" by John Greenleaf Whittier.

Page 104—"Teach me to love thee . . ." From "Spirit of God, Descend upon My Heart" by George Croly.

Page 108 "When [this German artist] . . ." From *Conscience* by Wilhelm Mensching, p. 21. Pendle Hill Pamphlet 117.

Page 109—"Weep not, weep not . . ." "Go Down, Death" from *God's Trombones* by James Weldon Johnson. Copyright 1927 by The Viking Press, Inc., 1955 by Grace Nail Johnson. Reprinted by permission of The Viking Press, Inc.

Page 112—"Grow strong, my comrade . . ." Dedication to his wife by Will Durant in *The Story of Philosophy.* Simon & Schuster, Inc. Copyright 1926, 1927, 1933 by Will Durant.

Page 114—"O great in our dull world . . ." From *Iphigenia Among the Tauri* by Euripides.

"For my husband . . ." From *Beyond My Dream* by Carmen Heath Blanc, pp. 11-12. The Marchbanks Press, 1958.

Page 115—"When grief loses itself . . ." From "Grief into Beauty" by Carmen Heath Blanc in *Friends Journal,* March 1, 1963.

Page 116—"When I was young . . ." From "My World Was Wrecked Once" by Elizabeth Gray Vining in *This I Believe,* edited by Edward P. Morgan, pp. 183-84. Simon & Schuster, Inc., 1952. Copyright, 1952, by Help, Inc.

Page 117—"There have been times . . ." From *The World in Tune* by Elizabeth Gray Vining, pp. 105-7. Harper & Row, Publishers, 1954. Copyright, 1942, 1952, 1954, by Elizabeth Gray Vining.

Page 118—"Sixteen days after Jessie's death . . ." From *The Road Home* by James McBride Dabbs, pp. 169-74, 184. United Church Press (The Christian Education Press), 1960.

Page 121—"Our dependence upon events . . ." From "The Ethics of Reverence for Life" by Albert Schweitzer in *Christendom,* Winter issue, 1936. The World Council of Churches.

Page 122—"My experience of the past twelve months . . ." From *Things That Matter* by Bishop Charles Henry Brent, edited by Frederick Ward Kates. Copyright 1945 by Harper & Brothers. Reprinted with permission of Harper & Row, Publishers, Inc.

"Cowards die many times . . ." From *Julius Caesar* by William Shakespeare.